sin
less

The Christian's War Within

W. THOMAS WARREN

WIPF & STOCK · Eugene, Oregon

SIN LESS
The Christian's War Within

Copyright © 2009 by W. Thomas Warren. All rights reserved. Except for brief quotations in critical publications or reviews, no part of this book may be reproduced or transmitted in any form or by any means without written permissions from the publisher. Write: Permissions, Wipf & Stock, 199 W. 8th Ave., Suite 3, Eugene, OR 97401.

ISBN 10: 1-60608-942-0
ISBN 13: 978-1-60608-942-2

WIPF & STOCK Publishers
199 W 8th Ave Suite 3
Eugene, OR 97401

Rev 1

Unless otherwise noted, Scripture quotations are from The Holy Bible, English Standard Version® (ESV). Copyright © 2001 by Crossway Bibles, a publishing ministry of Good News Publishers. Used by permission. All rights reserved.

Some Scripture quotations noted by "NIV" are from The Holy Bible, New International Version®. NIV ®. Copyright © 1973, 1978, 1984 by the International Bible Society. Used by permission. All rights reserved.

Manufactured in the USA

Table of Contents

Preface	ix
Introduction	xv
The approach of this book	xvi
Reading, praying, being filled with the Spirit	xvii
Chapter One: God and You	1
Our inability and God's remedy	3
Mercy for the vile	7
The trouble with religious people	9
The Dark Guest in the age of selfishness	10
The content of the Gospel in selfish hands	12
Resolutions	14
Chapter Two: Selfish Christians	15
Defining selfishness	16
Pure love	19
A selfish Christian	21
Deception	27
Knowing and loving God	29
Resolutions	32
Chapter Three: Dichotomies and Divisions	33
The cross of Christ and the cross of the believer	34
Substitutionary and representative	36
Dead and alive	38
Love and selfishness	42
When you believe God is not good	44

Suffering with Christ	48
Resolutions	50
Chapter Four: The Triggers of Desire	**51**
Lust, greed, and pride	52
Romans 7 and desire	54
Pulling the trigger	55
Applying Romans 7	58
Triggers of lust, greed, and pride	60
Triggers, an operational manual	68
Resolutions	70
Chapter Five: Declaration of War	**71**
No singing in Hell	72
Christian warfare	74
God, the church, and the self	75
The war for holiness	79
Two fronts of our war	82
Sanctification	85
Humility	89
The Word of God your unfailing ally	90
The Holy Spirit your greatest helper	91
Resolutions	94
Chapter Six: Self-examination	**95**
Examine yourself	98
A two-sided mirror	99
The Lord's Table	99
Sin's secrets	103
The assurance of salvation	105
Passing the test	108
Self-examination and self-denial	109
Resolutions	110
Chapter Seven: Repentance	**111**
Repentance, crucial but not mandatory	113
Repentance and self-examination	114
Teaching our tongues to confess	119
Half-repentance	122

Future repentance	124
Resolutions	127
Chapter Eight: The Love of God, the Lordship of Christ, and the Will of God	**129**
The love of God	131
The enemy of God's love	132
The Lordship of Christ	134
Choosing holiness and loving God	135
The will of God	138
Freedom	140
Resolutions	142
Chapter Nine: A Humble Heart and a Holy Life	**143**
Holiness by way of hardship	144
The problem of sanctification	147
Suffering, sorrow, and sanctification	149
Deny yourself	151
Hope and victory	154
Resolutions	156
Appendix One: The War about Romans 7	**157**
Appendix Two: The Question of Meaning	**165**
C.S. Lewis and Owen Barfield	165
Meaninglessness and selfishness	167
Christianity and meaning	169
Why attack meaning?	170
Scripture Index	**175**
Bibliography	**181**

In Memoriam

Harold O.J. Brown
1933-2007

Amicus et Magister

Preface

Dante's *Divine Comedy* begins with a man lost in a forest, pursued by wild beasts, not knowing which way to go. He needs a guide to lead him out of the dark place. Without a guide, he would be lost.

Dorothy Sayers was my guide through this epic poem of 14,000 lines. It is the longest confession of sin and self-examination ever published. Reading Dante is difficult. His poem is about a journey laced with innumerable, unimportant details, complicated political intrigue, his own failed love life, and pot shots at local civic leaders and prelates who lived in 14th-century Florence. Dante began the *Comedy* in 1308. That aside, above all Dante's epic poem is an allegory about the Christian life and how to live it.[1]

It was the 19th-century Romantics who ignited a new interest in Dante within popular modern culture. Longfellow's 1867 translation of the *Inferno*[2] unlocked the Italian epic for American Romantics and philosophers. References to Dante began to spread exponentially across late 19th-century Romantic literature. Many who never would have read Dante in Italian became familiar with some of its characters and features through those works.

Almost 80 years after Longfellow's translation of Dante, Charles Williams wrote a seminal, almost mystical, work on Dante, *The*

---

1 Williams, *The Figure of Beatrice*, 176. "We have looked everywhere for enlightenment on Dante except in our lives and our love affairs."
2 Dante, *Inferno*, trans. Longfellow, 2003 (reprint of 1867 edition).

Figure of Beatrice (1943).³ Williams was a friend of Dorothy Sayers and a member of the Inklings (a group that included J.R.R. Tolkein, Owen Barfield, and C.S. Lewis). He became her first teacher and most quoted referent on *The Divine Comedy*. Sayers began with Williams, but she grew in her own love for Dante that sparked an obsession with *The Divine Comedy* that lasted from the early 1940s until her death in 1957.

Sayers wrote a new translation of the *Comedy* (in three volumes) with extensive historical and practical notes. She lectured extensively on Dante, and she wrote three other volumes of analysis, reflections, and wondering delight about what she had gleaned at Dante's feet.

Hell was published by Sayers in 1949, *Purgatory* in 1955. Sayers' last volume, *Paradise,* was not completed before her death. Barbara Reynolds finished Sayers' last volume of *Dante* in 1962.

Sayers published the first volume of *Introductory Papers on Dante*, Vol. 1, in 1954. In the year she died (1957), Vol. 2 of *Further Papers on Dante* was first published. Reynolds published Sayers' final volume of the papers, *The Poetry of Search and the Poetry of Statement: On Dante and Other Writers*, Vol. 3, in 1963. Sayers writes about the personal impact of the *Comedy*:

> I saw the whole lay-out of Hell as something actual and contemporary [writing in 1954]; something that one can see by looking into one's self, or into the pages of to-morrow's (sic) newspaper. I saw it, that is, as a judgment of fact, unaffected by its period, unaffected by its literary or dogmatic origins; and I recognised at the same moment that the judgment was true.⁴

---

3   Cf. Williams, *The Figure of Beatrice*.
4   Sayers, *Introductory Papers on Dante*, Vol. 1, 128.

The tiniest details, the shortest turn of phrase in the *Comedy*, often yielded wonderful illustrations of spiritual principles and practical insights about the trials and pitfalls of living as a child of God who longs to be holy. Sayers writes:

> It is the story of the way of the soul at all times. It is, for example, the way of the individual soul in *this* life. Hell, Purgatory and Heaven, is [note the singular] within the soul.[5]

In my study for this book, I would frequently read Sayers' *Dante*, and while reading it, I would often be so arrested by its content that I would be left to stand alone, as it were, gasping for air, brought on by the truthfulness of his confession, and the power of the allegorical pictures of the human heart. I would be stunned by my own heart's filth, duplicity, disingenuousness, or foolishness. What I read in him, I knew to be true in me. I had journeyed on my own way through Hell, Purgatory, and Paradise in the sense we are here describing.

This book began with Sayers on Dante. After that it became clear to me that ancient and modern authors alike had tread much the same path as Dante in the pursuit of God's holiness within the human heart. My studies lead me to Augustine, Pascal, John Calvin, the Puritans (Robert Candlish, Timothy Rogers, Walter Marshall, Jonathan Edwards, and others), the later Reformed writers (Martyn Lloyd-Jones, John Murray, Charles Spurgeon, B.B. Warfield, and others), the modern evangelicals (D.A. Carson, C.F.H. Henry, and others), and the contemporary Puritans (Michael Horton, C.J. Mahaney, John Piper, R.C. Sproul, and others). Many voices echoed this same, now-seldom-heard song about the beauty of holiness and the extraordinary difficulty we all face in living a holy life and of dying to sin.

Despite its insights, the *Comedy* is flawed. It is provincial, and it

---

5 Ibid., Vol. 1, 10–11.

is locked in a distant epoch, an imponderable politic, and an almost inaccessible ancient worldview. But Dante also displays unparalleled knowledge of his world, ancient literature, and the Scriptures. *The Divine Comedy* has universal appeal because the nature of people, sin, and salvation has not changed.

Dante's work also has much in it that Reformed, orthodox, and evangelical readers will find not merely arcane but erroneous. In *Paradise* you will find veneration of the Virgin Mary, inclusion of noble pagans in Heaven, and tastes of medieval worship that grate against Protestant sensibilities. One should not reject *Purgatory* because it mirrors Roman Catholic theology. Instead, one should accept *The Divine Comedy* because it is an allegory about sanctification and the Christian's war with sin. There is so much that is biblical, true, and honest, that the mistakes are all the more apparent. Dante was a product of his day, and we should not read him uncritically.

Its flaws aside, *The Divine Comedy* is an ecstatic, joyous, heart-wrenching, painfully honest guide through self-denial and true repentance that leads to the bliss of life in the presence of Christ. He grasped with a poet's imagination the map of the human heart and the way to salvation. Sayers writes:

> The truth of the *Inferno* is to be sought in the allegory and not in the literal story. The map of Hell is the map of the black heart; if we want to verify it, we cannot do so from books.

She continues:

> The kingdom of Hell, like the kingdom of Heaven, is within you.[6]

The *Comedy* is a poem about your heart. In it you learn about

---

[6] Sayers, *Introductory Papers on Dante*, Vol. 1, 130.

sin. You learn about those who are in Hell and why they clamor to go there. You see that religion, as such, does not keep one from sinning nor from being damned. And you see sin stripped from the lives of believers by the joyful, painful, and difficult means of purgation, Dante's allegory for the mortification of sins.

Then there is Beatrice, the glorious, beautiful, wise figure of blessing. She is grace. What beauty! What wisdom! What power! She is the grace that leads him through this life, just to the throne of God; through the sloughs and up the mountains, and brings him to Heaven, where the Christian yields his will completely to God's. C.S. Lewis writes about Christians who live the most for God:

> ... those who can say like St. Paul that for them 'to live is Christ.' These people got rid of the tiresome business of adjusting the rival claims of Self and God by the simple expedient of rejecting the claims of Self altogether. The old egoistic will has been turned round, reconditioned, and made into a new thing. The will of Christ no longer limits theirs; it is theirs.[7]

Living the Christian life is much easier when we learn by practical examples how to live a holy life. Dante is useful as a substitutionary guide to holiness. Until more people become holy, living obediently to God's will and dying to sin in practical and repeatable ways in our day, Dante may serve as a guide to the lives we should aspire to live as biblical Christians. When holiness has been restored to the lives of many Christians in our time, perhaps then we will be instructed by the beauty of their lives and by the example of their holy choices, their humility and honesty, and we will then have no further need for an ancient book about holiness.

We ought to live holy lives, not because a 14th-century poet wrote about it, but because the Word of God describes our lives in

---

7 Lewis, *Present Concerns*, 21.

this way. Sinning less must be part of living a holy life. This little book shares Dante's lofty purpose that Christians might sin less.

> Since we have these promises, beloved, let us cleanse ourselves from every defilement of body and spirit, bringing holiness to completion in the fear of God. (2 Corinthians 7:1)

> ... and to put on the new self, created after the likeness of God in true righteousness and holiness. (Ephesians 4:24)

> For God has not called us for impurity, but in holiness. (1 Thessalonians 4:7)

> ... since it is written, "You shall be holy, for I am holy."(1 Peter 1:16)

> Since everything will be destroyed in this way, what kind of people ought you to be? You ought to live holy and godly lives. (2 Peter 3:11, NIV)

Introduction

I was blameless before him,
and I kept myself from my guilt. (Psalm 18:23)

Destroy, O God, the Dark Guest within
whose hidden presence makes my life a hell. [1]

There is a great difference between being forgiven and being holy. It might be better to be shown—to be given examples of how to live—than to try to figure out for ourselves what holiness would look like in a human being. We may think that holiness is for God rather than his followers. Holiness, as a virtue separated from God, feels like phoniness or judgmentalism. When we think of somebody who is holy, we don't necessarily see it as a good thing. It feels odd, alien, and unlike a quality we would like to have in our lives. Holiness seems like a laudable concept, except when we see it in people who live ugly lives—critical, damning, and nit-picking.

True holiness is God-affirming, not self-affirming. The greatest Christians we know about could be described as holy—though they would never describe themselves in that way. We might have heard about some of these remarkable Christians that lived for God, gave everything to him, and served him faithfully. Some of these people sacrificed everything to follow Jesus Christ. William Borden and Jim Elliot jump to my mind. They are perhaps not well-known to

---

1 Bennett, ed. *The Valley of Vision,* 122.

younger readers. The difference between those truly "holy" people and us seems impossibly great.

This book is for people who know they could love God more, who desire to know God better, and who long to be able to do what God wants. But they are not so sure how to make progress in their faith toward those goals. They believe in Christ, but sometimes they really mess up. They feel as if they are always starting over. This book is for people like that.

This book is direct and plain spoken but not simplistic. These instructions require some of the most difficult choices a believer makes in order to love God, to walk with God, and to obey God. And there is no end to it, at least in this life. You make a choice to live for God one day, and you must make a similar decision the next hour, the next day, and for the rest of your life. These decisions are difficult and necessary because they go to the core of what is wrong with us.

Everyone who believes has these struggles. In fact, the most dangerous people are those who think they have sin under control. They don't, you don't, I don't. It won't happen until you breathe your last. But you can do better. There is no requirement—some duty written in stone—that you must sin in some publicly humiliating way, or that you are destined to hurt your family, or your church, or yourself, by what you do. If this book succeeds in helping a few of us from falling into "horrid sins," it will be worth the effort. Horrid sins are the ones that take other people with you when you commit them. Some sins touch people who love you; they might even hurt people you haven't met. Those kinds of sins must not even be named among those who are followers of Christ (cf. Ephesians 5:3).

The approach of this book

This book is about theology and how you are affected by what you think about God. Marrying what you think about God and how you live your life has been essential training for Christians since the time of the New Testament. Because you know who God is, you should live differently.

Our problem today is that a lot of us have been taught badly about God. Strange ideas about God, his love, and what a true Christian is are affecting the way we live.

Erroneous thinking about God invariably leads to bad living. It may not lead to rampant immorality, but it may lead to the toleration of immorality. It may not lead you to lie, but it may lead you to bear with lying as a choice that is not worth repenting. The second sins are worse than the first. God permeates every part of your life. Even when you are wrong about God, the truth about God is still in play. The Psalmist cried, "Where can I flee from your presence?" (Psalm 139:7).

If God loves you and he is holy, at some point in your Christian experience you should begin to live for God completely. You will still get your holiness wrong at some points. But every believer ought to become more holy because you are forgiven of your sins. Jesus Christ lives in you by faith. You received the gift of the Holy Spirit of God and you are being transformed more and more in your character to be more like God. These identifying marks of the Christian happen in you because God shares his character with you. When you love God, you become more like him.

Reading, praying, being filled with the Spirit

This book is filled with Scripture. I have read this text through dozens of times, and even though I know what it contains, when I have shoved past the Scriptures and just read the text, I came away empty. When I read the Scriptures again for the umpteenth time, it is the Scriptures that compel the inner conversation with God; it is the Word that gets through my self-deception and refusal to be honest with God about who I am and what I have done.

Some of the subjects you will read about are very painful. Early in Chapter One, "God and You," we study how vile each one of us is. Yes, I said, "vile." That word, like so many here, applies to me as well. In fact, the word was chosen, like so many other hard words in this book, because no other word would do. Fallen people are vile.

When that word is used, I am moved to bring that description of my nature before God in confession. Words in the Bible, words that great Christians (such as Augustine and Pascal) use about themselves, I take to heart. I have an inner conversation with the Lord:

Lord, I read that people who sin are vile. O God! I hate that word! It is too crass, too condemning of my heart. I hate that kind of language used about my life.

But Lord, when I am quiet before you, in comparison with you I see myself as more than vile. I see my sin as something you hate, that you judge in me, and—greatest mercy ever spoken!—that Jesus died for.

Dear Father, I accept your indictment of my evil heart, my selfish words, and my longings to own my little portion of the world and to claim it all without you, apart from you, and separated from your influence within me. O Lord, I AM vile.

Forgive me. Forgive my vile heart, my wicked words, my twisted longings, for Jesus' sake, I pray. And may I who am vile, become pure, spotless, and greatly assured of your love for me.

By Christ I ask this. Amen.

These prayers will be included along the way. Your prayers could follow these, as they are written with us both in mind.

The work of the Spirit of God is more difficult to quantify as part of reading a book. It is one thing to read Scriptures, to think about what great Christians from the past have said about our Christian journey, but when the work of the Holy Spirit is involved, we can't be so ordered. He does what he wants to do in us. He is Sovereign over our life of faith.

A pattern that has been most helpful in my journey to greater understanding of God's standard of holiness for my life is that I ask each day (with some days of neglect and boredom along the way) for the Spirit of God to fill me, to help me to be the man that he wants me to be. I ask him to teach me, to humble my pride, and to help me to understand and receive the qualities he wants to form in me. And then I spend time in yielding myself to the Spirit's filling, almost at a physical level, sighing quietly, remembering my need and weaknesses, declaring my failure at pleasing God apart from his help and strength, and acknowledging my grotesque failures in the past at trying to live for him in my own power.

I could not quantify any mystical experiences that would make it into a journal, but there does come a conviction to keep at it, a calming force to keep me still longer, an appropriating need to pull the Word inside my heart and to keep it a part of my life for more than a moment.

If you would pray for the Spirit's filling before you read, perhaps the Spirit could take God's Word, and even some of these words, and do a work in you that would be worth more than the price of a book written by a small-town pastor who has been trying to walk with God for a long time but who has succeeded in walking with God only when he knew he couldn't do it alone.

Chapter One

God and You

For the love of Christ controls us, because we have concluded this: that one has died for all, therefore all have died; and he died for all, that those who live might no longer live for themselves but for him who for their sake died and was raised. (2 Corinthians 5:14–15)

What a long way it is between knowing God and loving him ... [1]

Anyone with even the slightest religious consciousness must be afflicted from time to time by the contrast between his religious faith and his behavior. [2]

Humility is required of all who come to God.[3] It is wonderful to know God's love. It is also a crushing experience. God's love is directly connected to who God is. God is in charge of everything, including you. He rules without your permission. He has a will that almost always departs from what you want or love. He is free to change your life by events you do not control. He redefines every relationship. He is invasive, intrusive, and uninvited. And he is loving, redemptive, merciful, and wise.

Coming to God, you are overjoyed with love and forgiveness, but you are also reminded of who you are and what you have done to other

---

1 Pascal, *Penseés*, trans. Krailsheimer, Sect. 280, p. 137.
2 Eliot, "Notes Toward the Definition of Culture," *Christianity and Culture*, 103.
3 Calvin, *The Institutes of the Christian Religion,* 2, 2, 11, pp. 268–269, quoting Thomas Chrysotom, " ... the foundation of our philosophy is humility," *De profectu evangelii.*

people and to God. The joy of your salvation is quickly changed to an embarrassing awareness of yourself that feels like powerlessness, inability, and moral ugliness. It is terrifying to come to God. And it is the only way to peace. Humility is knowing God, and then understanding yourself. Thinking about God causes you to think less of yourself.[4]

When you came to God, you might not have understood that knowing God always comes with a heavy price. Something in you has to give. Contemplating God changes how you think about everything. It affects every choice you make. It both arrests your emotions—constraining them to obey God's will—and liberates them, focusing your passions, loves, and longings on God. Knowing God disrupts every thought you have about yourself. It changes how you understand every other truth you know. It infects every longing and choice. Knowing about God, you must either love him as God or hate him as God. Ambivalence is not possible.

"God"—the very word defines the universe as his creation, and it defines you as a dependent part of that universe. God lives. The inarguable fact of his life determines where you come from, and what you are capable of. The existence of God limits you in severe ways. Because God exists, knows, and is good, you can't do all you desire to do. You can also unflinchingly examine who and what you love in light of who God is. Nothing about you or within you is hidden from God.

You are sometimes compelled to live a more moral life because you know that God sees, hears, and knows you completely. Knowing God makes you better.[5] But there is something in you that allows this pervasive thought about God to be tossed aside.

Sometimes you forget completely that God knows and sees everything you do. You see people who do outrageous sins and they do them with abandon, taking no thought about God or what they might say to him when they die. But comparing yourself to them, you find that you are capable of forgetting God, too. Their catastrophes provide no limits to your excesses.

---

4 Ibid., 2, 2, 10, pp. 267–268.
5 Hodge, *The Confession of Faith*, 239.

You ignore the fact that God knows your thoughts and that hiding from God is, quite obviously, impossible. So while knowing God should make you better, there are times that knowing God seems not to matter to you at all.

Our inability and God's remedy

If Christianity is true, it will tell you the truth about God and the truth about you. The Christian life forces a shift in the way you see everything. Christianity has a specific approach to reality—a view of the world and of life.[6] In the 1970s this was a hot topic on college campuses. We talked about our world and lifeview, we suggested ways of implementing a Christian world and lifeview in American society. By the late 1970s, evangelicals dreamed of succeeding as a social force to apply the Gospel of Christ to race relations, economic disparities, spiritual life, and happiness. The pursuit of a Christian world and lifeview captured the passion of committed Christians to have that central commitment of their lives impact everything in their world and in their life. A Christian's world and lifeview would be instructed by the Scriptures, the history of Christian thought, and the nature of Christian community. The world and lifeview was a desire to live under the lordship of Christ in every area of life.

In the 1990s and on to the present day, the primacy of the self created a world and lifeview that has the individual at the center. The self is the measure of all things. The self is the measure of truth in matters of religious commitment. For example, the self can create a faith in which one accepts the forgiveness of sins and the hope of heaven, but completely rejects the moral strictures that the Christian faith places on every believer's life. People understand their world and life to be their own, defined by their individual opinions, personally selecting what is accepted and rejected about the nature of God, free from any historic sense of the Christian faith as a way to live in obedience to God. The Christian faith is re-created in any form the individual wants it to be. There is little regard

---

6   The German is *Weltanschauung*.

for the meaning of theological terms (Christ, salvation, holiness, etc.), because those terms are injected with completely new definitions. This would have worked out fine, except that God has his own world and lifeview and his *Weltanschauung* does not invite emendation or correction by people. God is not changed by your view of the world and of life.

Your time on Earth should be spent conforming more and more of your views about creation, people, families, your work, your moral choices, questions about purpose and values, around the simple reality that God exists and that he has a personal interest in everything you think, say, and do. God's *Weltanschauung* creates a profound humility in Christians and an overwhelming hope and joy based on God's love and his salvation. It does not invite theological inventiveness nor would it lead to immorality.

If you claim faith in Christ but create your own worldview, that worldview will result in the shipwreck of your life. If your worldview is injected with your own content, you are placing your view of the world and of life in conflict with the reality of God. If you live by your own self-created views about God, you are creating conflict between God's will as it lays claim to your behavior and your personal set of values that you forged so you could live your life the way you wanted. If you are a Christian, your claim to know God is in conflict with your corrupt *Weltanschauung*.

Your failure to take God into account as you created your own world and lifeview could not hinder God from personally correcting, chastening, and disciplining you as his child. God is not limited in any way from directly and sovereignly impacting your life through events you cannot control. He will be holy in the lives of his children. "You shall be holy, for I am holy" (1 Peter 1:16), is a statement of fact, not an invitation. Some day we will all see the world and life as God sees them.

Holiness of life begins with changing your view of God and his world, to a view that is based on the truth about God and his sovereign purposes in creation and in people's lives. Humility is based on reality, not self-deception.

Knowing God brings your selfishness into very sharp and humiliating focus. There is much about you that God condemns and judges. He reacts to you, not out of caprice or vengeance, but out of holiness and wisdom. His holy character is at odds with your sinful desires and embarrassing actions.

Those who know God learn to relinquish their wills to God's will. They learn to love the qualities in God heart so much that those qualities become formed in them. They are changed people. This change always comes, and it is relentless:

> ... by which he has granted to us his precious and very great promises, so that through them you may become partakers of the divine nature, having escaped from the corruption that is in the world because of sinful desire. (2 Peter 1:4)

God's presence draws attention to much that is out of balance, twisted, supported by lies, and inexcusable in you. Your insatiable selfishness, your need for significance, your addiction to praise, your need for love in its many forms, and all that gets out of control in you are brought to an end in the presence of God. Knowing God is devastating to the self, and it brings an end to your private world and lifeview.

Becoming a Christian, you begin to worship God. You begin to live less and less as though you were God. Much of what happens to you in life is about God, making it very clear that he alone is God in the universe. There is no other God than the LORD (Isaiah 45:21; Daniel 3:29). The vision of God's glory forms humility in every believer. Humility is required of all who worship God. At the point at which you come to know about God as God, he offers you himself and his love as Redeemer.

Pascal wrote that a "true religion" should "teach us about our inability and tell us the remedy as well."[7] It is the most revolutionary spiritual journey you can take to have your eyes opened at one moment to the depth of your sin, the viciousness of your selfish heart, and the depravity of the sinful self, and then at the next moment

---

7   Pascal, *Penseés*, trans. Krailsheimer, Sect. 205, p. 98.

to understand the love of God in Christ for you, to learn about the sacrifice of Jesus for your sins, to receive complete forgiveness for all you have done and for who you are. Then, as if there could be even more God could do for you, you receive the gift of God the Spirit to live within you. Along with the gifts of forgiveness and eternal life, you also receive God. God and his gifts are inseparable.

Jesus said that people who are saved are in the minority. "Those who find [the way to life] are few," he said (Matthew 7:13). Therefore people who know God and live for God appear to be rare. People who claim to know God but live for themselves appear to be much more common. God's plans for our lives always collide with our plans. His ways are not our ways (cf. Isaiah 55:8). The vast majority of people know a great deal about God, his divinity, his creative power, his majesty and kingly rule, but they don't seem to like him very much. On their own, people don't *desire* God.[8]

Knowing God's will and desiring it is not the same thing. Jesus prayed, "If it be possible, let this cup pass from me ...." This means what the Father wanted him to do, Jesus found extremely difficult and he wanted not to do it. If there were another way, he asked for a way out. If there were no alternative to this hard thing that the Father wanted, Jesus would do it, despite the fact that it required his suffering and death. You can alienate God by your disobedience to his will. It isn't your hesitancy to obey God that alienates you from him. Jesus hesitated and even bargained with the Father for a way other than the cross. God the Father's displeasure comes when you know God's will but refuse to do it. That refusal is sin.

> Holy Father! I expect you to love me. I depend upon your love for me. But I have selfishly treated your love for me with the sin of presumption.
>
> Your Spirit has stirred in me the desire, the longing, the

---

8   Piper, *Desiring God.*

deep conviction that I must not come to you merely for gifts, like a child begs candy from a parent—No!—but that I must come to you *more* as a son (or daughter), as one who loves you with a love unlike any earthly love; a love that you placed within me, but that I have not sought to grow within me, nor even to explore its dimensions and eternity in me.

Forgive me for treating your love so contemptuously; and for my greed to have all your favors for myself, but all the while I am enriched by you, I neglect you, my God.

I am so sorry that I have for many years lived as one who is blind when your light of love was shining as a Sun into my unseeing eyes. Help me to know what you want me to do; and then make me into the person who would never again refuse to do it. By Christ I pray this. Amen.

Mercy for the vile

You have lied, you have been selfish, and you have done things that you knew were morally wrong. You did these things because you wanted to do them. No one forced you. Vileness means that something bad is in you, tossed together with evil motives, and selfishness added to the mix. The word means that you are morally repugnant. That seems a bit harsh at first—that is, until you add up your actions. Our world is upside down. Augustine understood this:

> The world is upside down—what grieves us ought not, but what doesn't [grieve us] should.[9]

---

[9] Augustine, *Confessions*, trans. Sheed, Sect. 10, 37, p. 203.

Every new Christian must declare his sinfulness *before* he can become part of a Christian community. Every baptism rite declares that you are a sinner in desperate need of forgiveness. This acknowledgment of sin is where every Christian begins.

Knowing yourself is difficult because you are so vile. On the one hand, the Gospel informs you of your sin, and then it gives you, in some detail, the solution God created to punish your vileness. Christ died for your sin (nature), and for your sins (words, deeds, thoughts). You are given the promise of new life and the seal of the Spirit of God within you. But because of your sin, in spite of these promises, you still think better of yourself than you are. You are compelled to deceive yourself about your goodness.

The Gospel hits you hard with the truth about you, and then it tells you that God would condescend to live forever in you who believe! God lives in those who love him! More from Pascal:

> Incredible that God should unite himself to us. This consideration derives solely from realizing our own vileness, but, if you sincerely believe it, follow it out as far as I do and recognize that we are in fact so vile that, left to ourselves, we are incapable of knowing whether this mercy may not make us capable of reaching him.[10]

Your vileness has so twisted your perceptions you cannot grasp your own incapacity, blindness, and ignorance of your perilous condition as a sinner. Sin makes you doubly blind: You can neither fully grasp how horrid your sin is, nor comprehend that God desires to be merciful to you. God gave you the faith you needed to grasp his loving intentions toward you even before you were saved (cf. Ephesians 2:8). It was God's gift to you. God redeems vile people, spiritually dead people.

---

10 Pascal, *Penseés*, in *Devotional Classics*, eds. Foster and Smith, 145.

The trouble with religious people

Religious people use their righteous acts to perfume the stench of their sin. They believe their rites and traditions are from God and that's all he requires of them. Many are content to play at religion their entire lives and never have the slightest sense that the holiness of God, the majesty of his person, the perfections of his will, or the certainty of his coming reign should lay claim to their souls absolutely. The thought that God would execute his righteous judgment on every sinful whisper, every heinous slander, every dirty thought or deed, every thoughtless, proud, presumptuous religious act, and every failure of love has been denied by them so much so that they will not think of their failures until the day of coming judgment. Denial of one's sins also requires a denial of God. Those who do not think about God are in great peril.

When people try to be "good," they mess it up. Your righteousness is imaginary, exaggerated, or incomplete. Righteousness is a game you cannot win. When you try to be good, you can't be good enough. When you try to love, you love imperfectly. You sacrifice for someone precious to you and yet some foul part of your heart wants a reward for what you did, some praise or *quid pro quo*. This is why religious people are so discontent, damning, or hypocritical.

Your unrighteousness is just as confused. You do something bad and you think, "That wasn't too bad." Or by obscene arrogance you place yourself beyond God's power to forgive and with disgusting pride you utter something like, "God could never forgive me for what I did." Do you think your sin is stronger than the grace of God?

This war has many battlefields. You could compare yourself with someone worse than you by saying, "At least I'm not a murderer, or a druggie." Or with plastic humility compare yourself with someone you think is better than you by saying, "No matter how hard I try, I will never be as good as Bob (Mary, etc.)." Your scales of measurement are not accurately set to truth. It is not what you think about you that matters.

Repentance is much harder than apologizing or making an

excuse. Repentance is confessing the sin, turning from it, and vowing with every fiber of your being not to do it again.

An assertion of your goodness stands at enmity with Jesus' death. He didn't spill his holy blood because you were a nice person. Jesus Christ died for sinners. It was ugly, unimaginably difficult, and inexpressibly wonderful that Christ would come to "seek and to save the lost" (cf. Luke 5:32; 19:10). You were lost. He found you.

A vile person can be humbled—a religious person, not so much.[11] The Savior came for the sick, the dead, the blind, and the famished. Not for the good, the righteous, or the perfect. People who are forgiven become meek, humble, servant-hearted, self-effacing, surrendered, and gladly obedient. They know they are vile but are now saved by God's mercy—his unbelievable, undeserved, unqualified *mercy*. Only the humble can love God and serve him.

If you think you don't need a bleeding Savior suffering the wrath of Almighty God in your place, then the Christian faith is not for you.

The Dark Guest in the age of selfishness

You are selfish. People in China, the United States, and Latvia are selfish. The best person in the world (apart from Jesus Christ) is selfish. It is a tautology—a self-defining, self-evident truth—that everyone is selfish. Certainly, some are more selfish than others. Some are more overtly selfish than others. Some are more destructively selfish than others. Not everyone becomes a mass murderer or an adulterer. Even nice people do some bad things. No one is holy but God.

Examples of sin in others prove nothing about you. Your battle is not about what others do; it is about what you do. Sayers writes:

> ... we see that the mere existence of a "self" that

---

[11] Cp. Edwards, *The Works of Jonathan Edwards,* Vol. 1, Resolution 8. "To act, in all respects, both speaking and doing, as if nobody had been so vile as I, and as if I had committed the same sins ... as others ...."

can in a real sense know itself as "other than" God, offers the possibility for the self to imagine itself independent of God, and instead of wheeling its will and desire about him, to try and find its true end in itself and to revolve around that.[12]

People are selfish. Your life is like the lives of millions of other people—when the truth about you is told, when your gossip is revealed, your lies uncovered, your theft exposed, your hypocrisy displayed, when your neglect of a friend destroys a precious friendship, when your dalliance is made public and breaks the hearts of people who love you. You should be doing something about your personal, all-pervasive, undeniable selfishness.

Selfishness is accurate and illuminating shorthand for indwelling sin. Some Puritans called indwelling sin the "Dark Guest." That name captures how personal sin cunningly entices your heart to fulfill your desires. Sin is a power of self-directedness that works in opposition to God and his will. That personal power of sin is subtle, incessant, and devastating to your spiritual life.

Sin is an alienating, relationship-breaking force that separates you from and damages your connection with God. Indwelling sin wages war, enslaves, blinds, lies, and it destroys your life. Sin convinces you that good is evil and that evil is good. When you sin, you believe in it. Sin corrupts and enslaves. It lies and it kills. Sayers writes:

> ... the knowing of good as evil—is what is known as Original Sin: and it is plain enough that we are in fact all born with it, however we come to be so.[13]

You have good and evil competing for your heart. This is an epic struggle. You are holy and wicked. You are inclined to love

---

12 Sayers, *Introductory Papers on Dante,* Vol. 1, 62.
13 Ibid., 66.

God and resent him. You want to do evil and worship God. You want to be holy and do your own will instead of God's. You are double-minded.

The Christian is a saint (holy by Christ's work on the Cross) and a sinner (one who breaks God's law and defies God's will). Martin Luther described the Christian as "simultaneously justified and a sinner." [14]

God sees the heart. He pays attention to your actions. He is not impressed by words. The Christian life is lived by your actions, choices, and convictions. What you do reveals your desires.

The content of the Gospel in selfish hands

Selfishness, more than any other single factor today, is destroying effective ministry, polluting church leadership, and alienating God's people from each other. Selfish Christians miss God and his blessings for the local church. This sin is antithetical to holiness. God hates it.

True Christians are loved by their friends and followers more over time, not less. The more you get to know them, the more you see they know their weaknesses, their sin, and their need of a Redeemer. They are quick to repent, and eager to confess and forgive. They are overwhelmingly grace-filled and they are vessels of the love of God to others. They need to impress no one. They live supremely for God alone. Timothy Rogers writes:

> This esteem is not wrought by a hasty glance or a passing view, but by deep thoughtfulness, attended with calm and sedate reflections on our own guilt and his mercy; on our own emptiness and miseries and his all-sufficiency. It then comes from balancing all things that pretend to a share in our affections

---

[14] Luther, *Lectures on Romans,* ed. Pauck, 193ff. (Romans 7); and xliv in the Introduction. *"Simul justus et peccator."*

and submitting at length to the greater claim of God .... [15]

O God who is greater than my sin, my soul is divided within me. I love you for your love for me and then I hate you when you show me I must give up some delicacy of my lusts if I am to follow you. I have two minds and two hearts. I can think of you one moment and utterly forget you the next, depending on what I desire to do. Help me, O God!

Every one of my sins is a sin against your love for me. All my desires seek my joy outside of you, hoping to satisfy my heart and my mind only in myself. When I sin against you, I have left you and lost you, my Rescuer.

I have exchanged your personal presence for pleasure and have cast moments of amazing closeness with you, that came from your delight in my faith-filled obedience, into the garbage heap.

Unite my heart to love you completely. Destroy the division within my heart, and set your love in me. My love is a failure. By the love of Jesus I pray this. Amen

---

[15] Rogers, *Trouble of Mind and the Disease of Melancholy*, 260.

Resolutions

1. To examine my personal humility as an essential virtue in my heart, if I am to live for God.
2. To understand the difference between knowing God's will and doing it.
3. To know the great evil in my heart whenever I refuse to do the will of God.
4. To grasp my own vileness before God, who is holy.
5. To say of my sin what God would say of it.
6. To know that I am possessed of such self-deception that I can lie to myself about every aspect of my life with God and for him.
7. To understand how exalted or diminished is my estimation of myself.
8. To practice a true repentance that includes not only sorrow for sin but an absolute turning from it.
9. To know what it is to be a vile person who has been humbled before God's holiness.
10. To reckon myself to be a selfish man, though redeemed.
11. To determine to be a friend to others, for Jesus' sake, who is overwhelmingly grace-filled and a vessel of the love of God to them.
12. To live for God alone.

NOTE: A resolution is a commitment to truth or to a principle of Scripture accompanied by some decision or action to abide by these commitments and principles.

Jonathan Edwards wrote his own expanding set of resolutions and he continually renewed his commitment to them throughout his life, until the day he died.[16]

---

16 Edwards, *The Works of Jonathan Edwards*, Vol. 1, xvii–xxiii.

Chapter Two

Selfish Christians

If you have this favor of God, you will easily look through all the painted varnish of the world and see its real vanity. God and divine things will not only gain your hearts, but gain them in a sovereign and powerful degree.

... Oh, give me not my portion in this world, but leave me have an inheritance in that which is to come. Let others pursue their various projects, and obtain what they pursue; let them succeed in their affairs.

... It is God whom I seek; it is he whom I most value.[1]

A Christian *should* value God the most. It is most natural for a child of God to trust his heavenly Father and to obey his will. How is it, then, that some believers live such ugly lives? Those believers can be unkind, full of gossip; a few even go to jail for terrible crimes. Valuing God isn't automatic and apparently it isn't easy either. A Christian may be forgiven, given a new life in Christ, be filled with the Holy Spirit, and yet, after all that mercy, still do terrible things! How can this be?

A selfish Christian thinks about his desires, wants, and needs. He is willing to use others, even God, to get what he wants. He is focused on the here and now, rather than what comes after.

---

1   Rogers, *Trouble of Mind and the Disease of Melancholy*, 260–261.

Defining selfishness

The self is how you distinguish yourself from God and from other people. You think, will, and feel. You have cognition, determination, and emotions. But you are in conflict about what you think. You have made good decisions and bad ones. Your emotions draw you to love or to hatred, but you do not love what is good, nor hate what is bad. You have a complex of forces, powers, and influences working within you. You can worship yourself, you can deceive yourself, and you can indulge yourself.[2]

Selfishness is certainly a sin (cf. James 3:14 and 16). It is a sin much like pride. But the self is much more complex than the sin of selfishness. The "self" describes the totality of the human person. You are a self. Your self relates to other selves. But your self is divided. If you are a believer, you have a new self and an old self within you.

Your thinking can be directed either by your new self or by your old self. Likewise, your will and emotions can be influenced by your Christian commitments or by your desire to resist God's will and do your own thing. A Christian can be selfless or selfish.

The Bible describes the conflict of the new self and the old self. Your new self is being created in the likeness of Christ. Your old self is your sinful nature that is being put off, resisted, killed (mortified) so that you might live more to God.

The New Nature:

> ... our inner self is being renewed day by day ....
> (2 Corinthians 4:16b)

> ... and have put on the new self, which is being renewed in knowledge after the image of its creator.
> (Colossians 3:10)

---

2 Cf. Elwell, ed., *Topical Analysis of the Bible*, 433–443.

> ... and to put on the new self, created after the likeness of God. (Ephesians 4:24)

The Old Sin Nature:

> ... but for those who are self-seeking and do not obey the truth, but obey unrighteousness, there will be wrath and fury. (Romans 2:8)

> We know that our old self was crucified with him .... (Romans 6:6)

The *old sin nature* we call the "old man," the "old self," "selfishness", the "inner self," the "sinful nature," "indwelling sin," the "law of sin," the "Dark Guest," and similar terms. Robert Mounce wrote about sin igniting conflict within the human heart:

> [The law of sin] was at war against his desire to obey the law of God .... So what I am by nature is in conflict with what I aspire to be as a child of God in whom the Spirit of God dwells.[3]

Indwelling sin is presented particularly in Romans 7 as an imprisoning, almost personal principle within the believer—"but I see in my members another law waging war against the law of my mind" (Romans 7:23). Augustine writes about the disturbing, defeating presence of sin as a *present-tense* struggle:

> [Paul] sees it in there, not remembers that it was there. He is pressed by what is present, not recalling the past. And he not only sees the law warring against him but even taking him captive to the law

---

3   Mounce, *Romans*, 170.

of sin, which is (not was) in his members.[4]

Augustine identified the ongoing, deadly conflict with sin that every Christian experiences with what we call the Dark Guest.

Selfishness, in modern culture, is useful shorthand for the set of besetting sins fueled by your fallen nature that still influences your thoughts, will, and feelings. You find, as Paul did, that a resistance, a struggle, a war is being waged within you that is pitting your desire to serve and worship God against a powerful, intelligent, conniving, lying power that lives within your very soul. The Dark Guest wages a war within you to keep you from doing God's will.

E.J. Carnell writes about this war against indwelling sin in the work of Søren Kierkegaard. Kierkegaard defines "being" as that point in your faith where you yield to God's will and choose to be in submission to him. But there is an inner conflict that makes doing God's will very difficult:

> The last stage in the religious life is that act of self-annihilation in which the ideal task of *being* an existing individual and the impossibility of fulfilling it concretely war against each other.[5]

Jesus and Paul both thought about sin in terms of a violent conflict:

> ... if your hand or foot causes you to sin, cut it off and throw it away .... (Matthew 18:8, NIV)

> In the same way, count yourselves dead to sin but alive to God in Christ Jesus. (Romans 6:11, NIV)

---

4 Augustine of Hippo, *On Nature and Grace,* 55, 65, in Oden and Bray, *Ancient Christian Commentary on Scripture,* 196.
5 Carnell, *The Burden of Søren Kierkegaard,* 134.

> I have been crucified with Christ .... (Galatians 2:20, ESV)

> If we died with him, we shall also live with him. (2 Timothy 2:11, NIV)

Selfishness is a manner of thinking, willing, and feeling that is produced by indwelling sin. Sin is what the Dark Guest plants, waters, and reaps. Sinning less would necessitate that you think, choose, and feel differently than when you are yielding to your sinful desires.

Selfish people worship man (cf. Isaiah 44:9–20). If your indwelling sin-nature twists God into your own image, your loves will also be idolatrous. As selfishness twists your view of self into a god, you can find yourself worshiping a man-sized god. Your sinful self cannot worship God by self-emptying, self-sacrifice, self-denial, servanthood, and selflessness. This personal evil infects souls so they become self-aggrandizing, self-serving, self-praising, and self-worshiping.

The self-worshiping are the most fragile, defensive, harsh, hostile, vindictive, unforgiving, pity-seeking, blame-casting, excuse-creating, and consequence-avoiding people on the planet. Pascal writes:

> Selfishness is universal; there is no remedy for it in ourselves.[6]

Pure love

God's love is pure, selfless, holy, and redemptive. Selfish people cannot love with God's love. God created people, not that they might worship themselves, but that they might give God the worship and glory that he deserves as God. God alone is to be worshiped as God.

---

6   Pascal, *Penseés*, trans. Krailsheimer, Sect. 205, p. 98.

> I give thanks to you, O Lord my God, with my whole heart, and I will glorify your name forever. (Psalm 86:12)

> ... bring my sons from afar and my daughters from the end of the earth, everyone who is called by my name, whom I created for my glory, whom I formed and made. (Isaiah 43:6b–7)

> So, whether you eat or drink, or whatever you do, do all to the glory of God. (1 Corinthians 10:31)

God's glory is a direct impediment to your self-fulfillment. God's love exposes your loves as selfish, empty, and essentially loveless. The selfish will not sacrifice unless there is some kind of advantage for them. Sin's personal presence within you asks: "How will this help me?" "What is in this for me?" "What will I gain in return for my acts of kindness?" Human love devolves into a theater for the selfish to advertise for their needs to be met, instead of a relationship of giving and sacrifice to another who is valued for who he is, not for what he has done. Human love wants everything, pays nothing, and seeks glory in man. Human love apart from the love of God is disgusting, often degrading, and disturbingly ugly. It rarely thinks of itself as ugly.

Biblical love, *agape*, is selfless, self-forgetting, self-sacrificial, Christlike, immensely costly, beautiful beyond words, and otherworldly. God acts to purge a Christian's love. He pours his love into your heart (cf. Romans 5:5).

God's love is eternal, sacrificial, unconditional, wise, limitless, pure, and just (eminently moral), derived from nothing in man, but completely from God's own heart. His love is humbling to everyone who receives it. Human love is self-serving, blind, limited, conditional, seeking peoples' praise, calculated, demanding, reciprocal, and immoral.

Your love needs to be purged, purified, and sanctified. God

indicts human love as a failure. Dante, as every Christian, was desperate for his love to be made pure. Sayers comments:

> Since every sin is a sin of love, the purgation of love itself is a part of every man's penitence.[7]

The Christian who walks with God experiences the purification of his loves. The Christian learns how to love. God's grace leads him, like Beatrice led Dante, to explore the breadth and length and height and depth of the love of God, that he might *know* God's love (cf. Ephesians 3:19). A pure heart can love others:

> Having purified your souls by your obedience to the truth for a sincere brotherly love, love one another earnestly from a pure heart. (1 Peter 1:22)

A selfish Christian

Christians love God and people. "We love because he first loved us" (1 John 4:19). A selfish Christian is nonsense. Knowing God makes selfishness and self-deception irrational. Selfish people will do almost anything to avoid the pain of self-examination, because they deny their sin, and they somehow convince themselves that they can hide it from God.[8] Self-examination and God-examination are closely related because both are rooted in the truth. The truth about you will lead you to the truth about God. The truth about God will define the truth about you.

Where will you hide from God? How will you avoid *God-examination*? Does God not see your life? Does God not know everything about you? Where will you hide from God? Where will you run from his presence? (cf. Psalm 139:7). One of the scariest thoughts in the Bible is that God knows you (cf. Luke 16:15).

---

7   Sayers, her commentary on Dante, *Purgatory*, 285.
8   Peck, "Healing Human Evil," in Zweig and Abrams, eds., *Meeting the Shadow*, 180.

Here are some descriptions of selfish people:

Selfish Christians are heretics.[9]

They affirm false doctrines as true. They deny that God alone is to be worshiped. Jesus may well say to them, "Depart from me, I never knew you" (Matthew 7:22–23). Their errors come from their sinful hearts.

The selfish redefine God's nature and character.

The selfish ascribe to God characteristics that God does not claim for himself. Neo-Platonists and Progressives created new concepts of God that have little bearing on God as he is—the God of creation, revelation, and redemption. People like to be inventive, especially about God and his dealings with people. However, inventiveness in theology is never a virtue. God is who he is. The selfish deny the authority of God's revelation about himself.

The selfish may desire to be in the place of God in worship, in control, and in self-determination.

They believe in themselves and not in God. They may use God-talk, but they reject the content of the Gospel of Christ that condemns human nature, deeds of righteousness, and goodness. They see themselves as more than good—as divine, even godlike. They even see God as their servant. They deny that matters of truth and justice reside in God's character alone. They believe they can define right and wrong. They are wrong.

The Christian worships God, understands he is not in control of his life, and submits to God as God.

The selfish may love God as a source of meaning but not as the Good.

The selfish seek God as a means to understanding, happiness, peace, or Heaven. The selfish worship God to gain a benefit from him.

---

9 Williams, *The Figure of Beatrice*, 126.

But God is worthy of worship solely because he is God. As the greatest good, loving God is higher than everything else one might do.

Christians give everything to God even when they lose everything in order to follow him.

The selfish may attempt to live a holy life, but they hate God's law.

The selfish often have a high moral life. Some are ascetic or punctilious in their ethics. But they are selective of God's law, picking only what is expedient or useful to them. They do not accept that the law is a practical expression of God's character. The law convicts all of humanity because it is a measure of God. So they obey the law superficially. Apart from Christ, the law of God crushes everyone.

The selfish may clamor to go to Hell, where the fear of punishment is turned into desire.

Hell is described by Dante as a place where people overcome their fear of punishment in pursuit of their desires. The selfish do not consider the judgment of God against their sins while they are caught in the snare of lust.

The righteous, however, have exchanged fear of punishment for the love of God.

The selfish may accept the church, but not its doctrine.

The selfish may love the emotions, ceremonies, frivolities, order, pomp, and austerity of the church. Something in the gravitas of church worship and work is appealing to the selfish. They are drawn to the congratulatory aspect of church life. They tolerate the inanities and endure the reasonlessness of much that occurs so they can be valued by those who attend. The selfish seek ways to aggrandize themselves. The church is a great place to exalt people, especially if the doctrine and mission of the church are shredded.

Holy people love to worship God in the company of others who love God. They love his law which is written on their hearts.

The selfish may try to find grace apart from God.

The selfish may depend on grace, but not the grace of God. They create gratuitousness, a false grace that accepts any sin and any sinner.

Selfish grace is indiscriminate, purposeless, and vague. The grace of God is God-focused, gloriously centered on Jesus Christ, and rejects all human virtue. The selfish use grace as a license to commit any sin. They believe another gospel and in another kind of grace. People in the world are confused about the nature of true Christianity because the selfish have redefined God and misused grace. The result is that they live ugly lives.

The holy do not presume upon grace. They worship God according to God's invitation and strictures. God's *transforming grace*[10] changes hearts, cleanses sin, and makes men and women new. Grace lives in holy people. It is their greatest Spirit-supplied resource for the Christian life.

The selfish may claim more righteousness than they have.

The selfish may believe themselves to have true righteousness, when what they have is a form of godliness that is alien to holiness.

> ... having the appearance of godliness, but denying its power. Avoid such people. (2 Timothy 3:5)

They exaggerate their goodness and measure themselves by other selfish individuals, rather than against the measure of the stature of Christ. The selfish may not praise their righteousness, but they believe in it.

The righteous know their sin and cry out against it. The holiest men on Earth are strikingly aware of their sinfulness. Rather than hiding their sins, they contend against them daily.

---

10 Bridges, *Transforming Grace*.

The selfish may have a righteousness that does not substantially change them.

The selfish may have a superficial, false, failing, unsavory righteousness that is achieved through comparison with other people or through a subtraction from God's character and work. Their righteousness rests in the rules of men. They do not have changed hearts because they have hearts of stone (cf. 1 Samuel 25:37; Job 41:24; Ezekiel 11:19, 36:26; cp. 2 Corinthians 3:3). They use righteousness as a form of flattery. But this is not a true righteousness at all.

The truly righteous make progress in holiness. They are a changed and ever-changing people (cf. 1 Thessalonians 4:1, 10).

The selfish may see love as an injustice, not as the greatest justice.

The selfish may cry out against God's love and true human love as being terribly unjust. They may believe that Heaven, in its free grace and unconditional forgiveness, is unjust. They claim a right of entry because of their works and goodness. They may protest that the cross and Hell are equally unnecessary. They protest against both the means of salvation and the wrath of God.

The cross of Christ is the satisfaction of the justice of God. True love is just.

The selfish may forget the end of life.

Francis of Assisi writes:

> Keep a clear eye toward life's end. Do not forget your purpose and destiny as God's creature.[11]

The selfish do not anticipate their own demise; they deny its

---

11   Francis of Assisi, *Letters to the Rulers of People*, cited in Manning, *The Signature of Jesus*, 66.

inevitability. Rather than living as people who will die and give an account to God, they live disconnected from their certain destiny and coming judgment. "For we must all appear before the judgment seat of Christ ..." (2 Corinthians 5:10).

Humility, for the righteous, grows from the seed of our certain death.

The selfish may put their virtues on the outside and vices in the heart.[12]

The selfish may keep their virtues in words and superficial deeds for others to hear and see, while they store vile vices deep within their hearts, where they coddle and nurse them in secret.

The righteous, by contrast, keep their virtues on the inside and their vices at the foot of the cross.

The selfish may see repentance as unnecessary.

The selfish may practice repentance as a religious form, but it is without substance. Repentance is a means of securing God's favor rather than putting off sin. They believe they should model repentance for others who need it. They do not renounce or turn from sin. They do not put sin to death.

By contrast, the holy examine even their repentance. A Christian will repent of selfish repentance.

> Therefore, since we are surrounded by so great a cloud of witnesses, let us also lay aside every weight, and sin which clings so closely, and let us run with endurance the race that is set before us. (Hebrews 12:1)

The selfish may not distinguish between love and its object.

The selfish believe that any kind of love is good. Moral choices are evaluated by the test of love: They are thought to be right if they

---

12 Lewis, *The Screwtape Letters*, 28.

are loving.[13] But love can be a very bad thing. The selfish seek the affection of others but not the affection of God.

Love is judged by its subject and its object, and the end to which it is aimed. The godly person knows that love is from God, it is essential to God, and that apart from God all loves are inferior, destructive, and damning. Human love always fails (cp. 1 Corinthians 13:8).

Deception

It is common for you to think you have understood a part of the doctrine of the self (e.g. "self-deception") only to discover that self-deception itself was at work blocking your attempt to understand it! But God is greater than your soul!

> But exhort one another every day, as long as it is called "today," that none of you may be hardened by the deceitfulness of sin. (Hebrews 3:13)

> The Word of God is living and powerful, piercing to the dividing of soul and spirit and joint and marrow, and is a discerner of the thoughts and intentions of every heart. (Hebrews 4:12)

Selfishness takes the various virtues (love, generosity, kindness, etc.) and it turns them into something similar to those virtues but with different motives or ends. One who is selfish is capable of a sort of love, but there is a calculation to it (i.e. "What will this get for me?"). The generous person will give to noble causes but says to himself, "People will think I am an example of a great and good person." And the angels are nauseated.

Christians can be selfish when they turn the Gospel of Jesus Christ into a system that brings them some result they value.

---

13 Cp. Fletcher, *Situation Ethics*, 5. A book that propounds the wicked thesis that whatever is loving is approved by God.

Perhaps they join a church to be better esteemed among their friends. Or they see God as now being morally obligated to answer their prayers, give them material goods, put them in successful businesses, or grant them physical health because they join a church, become a missionary or pastor, or sacrifice financially in some way (taking a low-paying job for the Lord, or give extra to a ministry, for example).

You can be selfish in your worship when you demand that the message make you happy, by wanting only the music that you like, by being critical of others in the room who are poorer or have some affliction, or by wanting the church to do things for you. Instead, you could come to church just to worship God.

By worshiping God and setting your selfish needs aside, you discover a much happier, more joyful worship. People are not compared, criticized, or gossiped about. They can now be loved.

You can be selfish in your prayers. God commands you to pray and delights in your prayers. When you call upon his name, he wants you to bring him all your needs and burdens. Prayer can be selfish when you want "not Thy will, but mine be done." It is possible for you to do Christian things, even duties that God has commanded, and do them not for God but for yourself. Murray explains the centrality of union with Christ if you are to live for him:

> Christians grow in obedience by the power of the gospel, not by their own strength. Christians are in union with Christ, and their Christian growth flows from this union, not from their own efforts. The Gospel is essential for growth in holiness.[14]
>
> Holiness comes from union with Christ ....[15]

---

14 Murray, Introduction to Marshall, *The Gospel Mystery of Sanctification*, 5.
15 Ibid., 6.

Walter Marshall writes about why so many fail in holiness:

> Many Christians fail in Christian living because they are satisfied with keeping only the external requirements of the law. They are very concerned about looking good on the outside, but they never learn how they can actually do true spiritual service to God from their hearts.[16]

Knowing and loving God

How can people who could not do God's will, become people who now do God's will from the heart? Assurance of salvation and love for God are the sources for true obedience and holiness. Marshall writes:

> Sanctification comes because the person truly wants to obey God. But no one wants to do good, or to obey God. How do we go from hating the good to loving it? From being one who desires no good thing, to being one who loves God above all and totally? ... True obedience means you love to obey God ...
>
> You have to be totally assured that you are reconciled to God and accepted by him.[17]

Assurance of salvation opens the door for confidence in prayer to God and for holy living because you know you are accepted in Christ. Obedience that flows from assurance is confident, courageous, and able to risk everything for God. The sinful self refuses to obey God. The new man yields in obedience to him. Your sinful

---

16　Marshall, *The Gospel Mystery of Sanctification*, 23.
17　Ibid., 27.

nature hates God's will. The new man loves and submits to it.

Why, then, is there this internal struggle in you? What purpose does it serve for you to struggle with sin? Why should every believer contend with this affliction? Why must you struggle so with this powerful foe? Edwards advised a young girl that there was a benefit in remembering her sin. A repentant sinner is humble, teachable, able to give and serve, to go and yield. You must remember your redemption. Here is Edwards:

> Though God has forgiven and forgotten your past sins, yet do not forget them yourself; often remember what a wretched bondslave you were in the land of Egypt.[18]

Perhaps a more tender purpose would be that God left your sin nature within your life to keep you tenderhearted toward the lost. By reminding you of your constant struggles with sin, you know that you are no different than those who are lost in their sin, except for the grace of Jesus Christ. Indwelling sin is a constant reminder of your need of the Savior and his Holy Spirit to comfort you every day you live on Earth. It is good to remember from what terrible sin you were saved (cf. Ephesians 2:11–22).

Redeemer of my Life, I cry out to you against my sinful nature. Its power has infected every molecule of my life. I have no friend, O God, no thought, no task that is untainted by my sinful heart, my selfish pride, my unteachable spirit. I am wearied by my sin's imaginations and enticements. In every thought and deed I find my sin. I cannot find one word or action that is pure within me. My sin is everywhere within

---

18 Edwards, "Edwards, Jon. Letter 1741 to a young lady residing in Smithfield, Conn.," Kistler, ed., *God's Call to Young People*, 224–229.

me, and it infects everything I am and do. O God, deliver me from this enslaving presence!

O Sanctifying God, teach me to give up all hope of making myself better. Remind me that, apart from your help, I will always fail, but with your glorious power, I am more than a conqueror.

Help me not despair in my repentance because I fail in all my promises to you. You are always faithful when I am not. Show me the poverty of my soul so I can love others who are as poor as I, while you are purging me of my much-loved sin. By Jesus Christ I ask this, Amen.

Resolutions

1. To think, will, and feel according to God's will and his design for my life.
2. To refuse to worship myself or to indulge myself.
3. To see my sinful self at war with the law of God.
4. To grasp my present tense struggle with indwelling sin.
5. To know that my selfish longings are at war against God.
6. To purge my love, to have a pure heart, and to know the love of God.
7. To be examined by God.
8. To trust in God's providence at all times.
9. To give everything to God, even if I lose everything for God.
10. To have no fear of punishment, because I am assured of the love of God.
11. To accept all that is orthodox and to reflect the truth of God's Word in my life, my choices, and in my loves.
12. To never presume upon grace, lest I selfishly sin against God.
13. To love the holiness of God.
14. To desire that God's holiness would change everything about me.
15. To have a humility that comes from the fact of my certain coming death and coming judgment.
16. To grow virtues deep within my heart and to keep my sins at the foot of the cross.
17. To be moved by God's love toward greater holiness in my life.

Chapter Three

Dichotomies and Divisions

> *In a sense, the supreme glory of the Christian life is that it gives us this wholeness, and delivers us from the dichotomies and the divisions which are ever characteristic of sin, not only as between man and man but even within the man himself.* [1]

> *Man is therefore nothing but disguise, falsehood and hypocrisy, both in himself and with regard to others.* [2]

Less sin in you would be a good thing. Who wouldn't want to sin less? There is no "one size fits all" to sanctification. One person will read the teaching in Proverbs 4 about guarding his life—his eyes, his lips, his heart, and his steps—and see practical instruction about holy living and living more for God. Another would read Proverbs 4 and park that teaching in the "interesting but not pertinent to me" part of his brain.

Time changes the way we read the Word of God. One year you read a line from Proverbs 5:22–23 that "the iniquities of the wicked ensnare him," and you yawn. A year later after you have been tied in knots in a trap with no escape, forgotten in some God-forsaken hole in a desert, you think, "I am trapped by my wickedness. I did *exactly* what Proverbs 5 warned me about." You see that God is working in time through your mistakes to bring you to the cross of

---

1   Lloyd-Jones, *Darkness and Light*, 202.
2   Pascal, *Penseés*, "Fragments from other sources," trans. Krailsheimer, 350.

Christ. That is where God deals with your sin. Every gift God gives you so you may sin less flows from the cross of Jesus.

If you are to sin less, you will spend more and more time thinking about the cross of Christ and you will begin to live your own crucifixion. You will take up your own cross and you will learn to die to your sin.

The cross of Christ and the cross of the believer

Without the cross of Christ there would be no Christianity. The cross of Christ is the very essence, the *sine qua non*, of the Christian faith. If there were no cross, no one would be saved. If a person does not receive the merits of the cross for his life, there is no redemption. The apostles held the cross as the central pillar of Christian theology. The cross is at the center of the New Testament.[3] Sinning less must always start at the cross.

Nothing is more precious to God's heart than the cross of his Son. But the importance of the cross is not limited to the redemption that Christ accomplished for us. The cross of Christ is also an example, a model for the manner of living of every Christian person. You bear your own cross.

Your cross can't pay the penalty for even one of your many sins. His cross saved sinners. Your cross leads you to become more like Christ in holiness and practical submission to the will of God. It is by taking up your cross that you learn to say, "Not my will, but yours be done." (Cf. Romans 6:8 and 2 Timothy 2:11.)

The holy life of every Christian flows from your being united with Christ in his death and resurrection. You are "crucified with him" (Romans 6:6) and have become "dead to sin and alive to God in Christ Jesus" (Romans 6:11). Holiness does not come to you by doing your will nor by neglecting God's commands. The requirements of God's will are difficult for you. They are contrary to the

---

3   Cf. Morris, *The Apostolic Preaching of the Cross*; and *The Cross in the New Testament*; and Denney, *The Death of Christ*.

desires of your selfish nature.

The ethical commands to live for God in holiness flow from your connection with your crucified and risen Savior. Peter draws the connection between the holiness of Christ and the holy lives of his followers:

> As obedient children, do not be conformed to the passions of your former ignorance, but as he who called you is holy, you also be holy in all your conduct, since it is written, "You shall be holy, for I am holy." (1 Peter 1:14–16)

Paul echoes the same theme:

> But thanks be to God, that you who were once slaves of sin have become obedient from the heart to the standard of teaching to which you were committed, and, having been set free from sin, have become slaves of righteousness. (Romans 6:17–18)

God doesn't compel you to obey his law. He sets you free from sin that you might obey him out of your love for God. The Spirit has filled your redeemed heart with the love of God that you might have a love for God and others. A Christian has freedom to love God and obey his will that an unbeliever cannot possibly attain, nor can an unredeemed person comprehend.

A Christian can now choose true holiness and actual righteousness. A believer's holy and righteous actions spawned by faith in the Redeemer are acceptable to God for Jesus' sake.

A believer also can be negligent, graceless, doubting, resistant to God's will, selfish, and prideful. Some Christians are very disobedient. They break God's law and resist God's will. Just because a Christian *can* obey God does not ensure that he *will* obey and yield his life as a slave of righteousness.

Substitutionary and representative

Christ has died for your sins. His death, therefore, is *substitutionary*. But his death is also *representative*.[4] His death is a model of your obedience to God. Christ was obedient to the Father unto death, therefore, you ought to be obedient to God by your death to sin and by your living to do God's will from the heart.

A believer looks to Christ's obedience as a model of his own obedience and servanthood (cp. Philippians 2:1–10). Your obedience will not be perfect. Though you are never fully "like Christ" in your obedience, nonetheless, his sacrifice, his condescension, his self-emptying, are compelling moral examples for you to obey God.

Christ's *substitutionary* sacrifice was not dependent upon human effort or permission. His death for sins was driven solely by God's grace and the display of God's glory to save sinners.

> We were buried therefore with him by baptism into death, in order that, just as Christ was raised from the dead by the glory of the Father, we too might walk in newness of life. (Romans 6:4)

There was clearly nothing in human beings that merited salvation, "… no one understands; no one seeks for God" (Romans 3:11). You deserved nothing but his displeasure, wrath, and punishment. This is true because you are not holy.

Christ's death is also *representative* of your Christian obedience. His death forms a pattern for how you yield to God in obedience. You are joined with Christ in his death, representatively, when you yield to God in true obedience to God's law and choose his will in daily obedience. By faith in Christ as Lord, you can live *more and more* like he lived.

---

4   Harrison, *The Expositor's Bible Commentary*, 68–69.

> ... that I may know him and the power of his resurrection, and may share his sufferings, becoming like him in his death. (Philippians 3:10)

These passages command the Christian to live according to the *representative* nature of Christ's life and death:

> ... just as Christ was raised from the dead by the glory of the Father, we too might walk in newness of life. (Romans 6:4b)

> Therefore welcome one another as Christ has welcomed you, for the glory of God. (Romans 15:7)

> And walk in love, as Christ loved us and gave himself up for us, a fragrant offering and sacrifice to God. (Ephesians 5:2)

> For the husband is the head of the wife even as Christ is the head of the church, his body, and is himself its Savior. (Ephesians 5:23)

> Husbands, love your wives, as Christ loved the church and gave himself up for her. (Ephesians 5:25, cp. 5:29)

By Christ's help, it is possible for you to be dead to sin. His power and victory are *capable* of freeing you from every temptation. You *could* love others as Christ has loved you. You *could* always walk in newness of life. The picture of what you *could* be is amazing and quite hopeful.

In spite of these possibilities, these potentialities, you sometimes do what God hates. Though you are redeemed, sin is still at work in your life. You could always resist sin, if you were perfectly obedient to God. But you do not always yield yourself to holiness. By faith in Christ you could please God in every choice you make, but some days you choose not to obey God. Your freedom permits choices that are selfish, sinful, and unholy. Indwelling sin continues to wage war within you.

> ... we too might walk in newness of life. For if we have been united with him in a death like his, we shall certainly be united with him in a resurrection like his. (Romans 6:4c–5)

Dead and alive

Before you came to faith in Christ you were under a death sentence because of your sins.

> And you were dead in the trespasses and sins in which you once walked, following the course of this world, following the prince of the power of the air, the spirit that is now at work in the sons of disobedience ... (Ephesians 2:1–2)

You were dead *in* your sins and incapable of saving yourself. Christ did for you what you could not do for yourself. Christ died for you, for your sins, because he loves you (cf. John 3:16). He suffered the terrible penalty you deserved. He died in your place (cf. Romans 5:8; 1 Thessalonians 5:10).

As a believer you are now dead *to* your sins (cf. Romans 6:4) because Christ now lives in you, giving you his power and victory over sin. You were justly condemned by God as a sinner who lived in your sins. As a believer in Christ, you are delivered from sin's power, both in terms of eternal life and forgiveness of all your sins, and in your choices. By Christ's sacrifice, you have his victory over sin's power and corruption. You are alive to righteousness and holiness. Everything you need is yours in Christ (cf. 2 Peter 1:3). A.W.

Pink writes:

> Everything which God requires from us, everything which is needed by us, is treasured up for us in Christ.[5]

Being dead to sin is not to be sin-free. It is to have victory over every sin, to be mastered by no sin, to be victorious in your battles, and to know with certainty that no sin can defeat you (cf. 1 Corinthians 10:13).

Christians sin. Sanctification and a holy life do not occur in the passive, the indifferent, the lazy, or the undisciplined. Sin is not defeated by the licentious or the self-deceiving. Sanctification is an active obedience accomplished by intentional compliance to the will of God empowered by the Spirit of God who lives within, under the authority of the Word of God.

The Scriptures are filled with commands for Christians to stop sinning, to move to maturity, to increase in holiness, to stop being immoral, and to stop gossiping, lying, and stealing. You have freedom as a Christian to resist and conquer every sin. You could, but you don't.

While on the Earth you live in conflict with your old sinful self. Sin has a corroding power in your heart and choices. Even though your redeemed self longs to please God and obey his will, you still sin. Every believer in Christ is both alive and dead at the same time: "I am crucified with Christ …" (Galatians 2:20). You are dead. "Nevertheless I live." And you are alive. "The life I now live in the flesh, I live by faith in the Son of God."

Some people who live badly are spiritually confused. They claim to be believers, but they do not know God and have not been redeemed from their sins, nor have they received the new birth. Their problem with sin is that they are not Christians.

Some may be spiritual infants who are dependent, immature,

---

5   Pink, *The Doctrine of Sanctification*, 144.

self-centered, and unknowledgeable. They sin because they do not choose to be holy. They do not read the Word; they do not obey God's law. They do not live morally pure lives in fidelity and chastity. They are ill-informed, undisciplined, disconnected, and selfish Christians.

A last group to consider are Christians who choose to sin. They are not simply ignorant or undisciplined. They are willfully disobedient and they knowingly reject God's law and his will for their lives. They know what is good and right and holy, but they do what is bad and wrong and filthy. They lose their assurance of salvation (cf. 1 John 2:29 and 5:13). They are cut off from Christian fellowship (cf. 1 Corinthians 5:2) and they bring dishonor to all who rightly follow Jesus Christ as Lord of their lives.

Some popular Christian writers propagate the notion that Christians are redeemed, forgiven, and saved, and therefore they are no longer sinners. They teach that you should never refer to yourself as a sinner because your true identity as a Christian is that you are "holy," "a saint." They have told only half the story, and they have seriously misunderstood the Word of God regarding the true nature of your war with indwelling sin and the commands of Scripture about living a holy life. Such an error in doctrine always brings moral disasters (cf. Romans 6:1ff., 7:20, 8:10, 14:23; 1 Corinthians 6:18; Ephesians 4:6; 1 Timothy 1:15, 5:20; James 4:8 and many others).

By not engaging in this personal war with indwelling sin, they are most vulnerable to its devastating influences.

> Do not present your members to sin as instruments for unrighteousness, but present yourselves to God as those who have been brought from death to life, and your members to God as instruments for righteousness. (Romans 6:13)

> So now it is no longer I who do it, but sin that dwells within me. (Romans 7:17)

Chapter Three: Dichotomies and Divisions

The sinful nature is slain by Christ's redemption—"We know that our old self was crucified with him" (Romans 6:6a)—and it is still present and influential in every believer (Romans 7:17). Your sinful self will compel you and deceive you to live as though you were still dead in your sins. Sin creates the corrupting fiction that you are powerless to overcome your desires.

But sin can be defeated at every turn. Every enticement to deny God, to speak with foul language, to act upon lust, to feed one's pride, or to take what belongs to others, can be overcome. Every invention of evil can be resisted and repelled. But the battle must be fought every day, in every decision, within you.

Your sinful nature creates fear, guilt, and shame. Under its influence you can become angry at God, frustrated with people, and rebellious against God's Providence, guidance, and promises. You can fail morally. Your faith can be weakened. You can be disobedient to God's Word. You can harbor an unforgiving spirit. You can grieve God's Holy Spirit who lives within you. You can neglect the duties and graces that would make you strong and effective. You can be cowardly and foolish.

Despite that powerful enemy within, God has given you his Word and his Holy Spirit, and therefore there is great hope and victory for every believer who wages war against indwelling sin! By the Spirit of God you can live a *true life in Christ*:

> … thus storing up treasure for themselves as a good foundation for the future, so that they may take hold of that which is truly life. (1 Timothy 6:19)

Timothy Rogers gives a good word of assurance:

> If you have this favor of God, you will know it by the hatred that you have of sin. Wherever this favor comes, it will banish sin; it will weaken and expel it. And though it does not altogether destroy your sin, yet it will take away from it all its former

amiableness and beauty. You will not sin with such boldness as you used to do; nay, you will be so far from doing so that you will not dare to commit the least iniquity. And if there is fixed in your souls a real and abiding hatred of sin, and if you use all good endeavors against it, it is a most certain mark that you have passed from death to life.[6]

This war between your sinful self and your redeemed nature creates conflict within you. The Spirit is mighty in you who believe, and you are promised his victory over any temptation (1 Corinthians 10:13). Your new creation is being conformed to the image of Christ. Your sin nature is being put to death. Your heart and your will are being made new. Richard Foster writes:

Do you know what a great freedom this crucifixion of the will is? It means freedom from what A.W. Tozer called "the fine threads of the self-life, the hyphenated sins of the human spirit." It means freedom from the self-sins: Self-sufficiency, self-pity, self-absorption, self-abuse, self-aggrandizement, self-castigation, self-deception, self-exaltation, self-depreciation, self-indulgence, self-hatred, and a host of others just like them. It means freedom from the everlasting burden of always having to get our own way. It means freedom to care for others, to genuinely put their needs first, to give joyfully and freely.[7]

Love and selfishness

Your conscience is powerless to constrain your sin. The conscience

---

6   Rogers, *Trouble of Mind and the Disease of Melancholy*, 261.

7   Foster, *Prayer*, 54.

can be silenced, confused, and made to serve your desires. When you are sinning you put the conscience on "mute." Your greatest sins were probably a lot of fun, taken in with hardly a word from your inner moral barometer. You did what you wanted and felt pretty much guilt-free until later, when the Spirit of God struck your heart for your terrible fall, crushing your duplicity and lies to God. When conscience is made alive by the Spirit, it may then be heard, but not before.

> To the pure, all things are pure, but to the defiled and unbelieving, nothing is pure; but both their minds and their consciences are defiled. (Titus 1:15)

David did not hesitate when he rushed to Bathsheba's bed. Later he grieved terribly over what he had done (Psalms 32 and 51). He was just like you when you fall into sin. Christians who fail and fall know this pattern: Do what you want; shatter your life to pieces; grieve over it until you die; and recover by grace as much as God may restore to you.

By contrast, Moses is said to have passed up the "fleeting pleasures of sin" (cf. Hebrews 11:29), because he saw something more lasting. You can be a David. Or you can be a Moses. It's up to you.

The sinful self says, "I am my own. I do not belong to God." Sin charges, "God cannot be trusted." It lies to us by saying, "You are not safe living by God's promises." Your sinful self's greatest ploy shouts, "God does not love you!" John Owen wrote:

> Let grace be enthroned in the mind and judgment, yet if the law of sin lays hold upon and entangles the affections, or any of them, it has gotten a fort from whence it continually assaults the soul.[8]

In spite of sin shouting in your heart, the Spirit of God confirms you in the love of God. The love of God is a flood of grace and mercy

---

8   Owen, *Overcoming Sin and Temptation*, 281.

that flows into your heart (cf. Romans 5:5). J.I. Packer writes:

> The love of God has flooded our inmost heart.
>
> ... It is especially the work of the Holy Spirit who gives this gift.[9]

When you believe God is not good

In Genesis 3, Adam and Eve believed the lie of Satan. He told them when they sinned against God that God's promise of sure, certain death upon that sin would not occur. Satan contradicted God, promising Adam and Eve, "You shall not surely die." Satan proudly promised them that if they rebelled against God's rule, they would become "like God," knowing good and evil (Genesis 3:4–5). Dante sang about the devastating consequences of our first parents' sin. He visualized Jesus in Mary's lap after the crucifixion:

> The wound which Mary tended and assuaged
> > Was by the beauteous person at her feet
> Inflicted in surrender so ill-gauged.[10]

Sin was "ill-gauged" in that its effects were catastrophic for humanity. It caused the fall of all nature and it brought spiritual death and physical death into the world. Sin was "ill-gauged" from the view of Heaven because it cost the Son of God his life. Adam and Eve's fear of God and their damning doubt of his blessings show how great was their unbelief about God's truthfulness and his goodness. They died spiritually because they believed the lie. Jonathan Edwards writes:

> Self-love became absolute master of [Adam's] soul,

---

9   Packer, *Knowing God*, 106–107.
10 Dante, *Hell*, trans. Sayers and Reynolds, Canto 32, 4–6, p. 334. Cf. Matthew 27:55, 56; and John 19:25.

and the more noble and spiritual principles of his being took wings and flew away.[11]

Walter Marshall writes:

When you have an evil conscience, you think God is your enemy.[12]

Dear heavenly Father, like Adam I doubt your wisdom and your love. Why else would I be afraid or feel abandoned? Your faithfulness has never stopped me from doubting whether your will would be good for me. I wonder, patient God, if what glorifies you could possibly be good for me.

I have bucked against your will. I have hated what you wanted me to choose. I have considered my way better than yours. I am like Adam, but in some ways worse. Because so many have gone before and they and lived for you alone, I have no excuse for my doubts. Why am I still am filled with unbelief even after I have declared my faith in you?

You bear with my evil conscience and instruct it. You allay my fears and quench my doubts. You shore up my weaknesses and you tell me the bald truth about what I need, not what I want. Your redeeming love lifts my eyes from my sin to your salvation. Your will becomes sweeter to my heart as you embrace me more and more fully in new life, new hope, and love made perfect.

---

11 Edwards, *Charity and Its Fruits*, 228; and Piper, *Future Grace*, 389.
12 Marshall, *The Gospel Mystery of Sanctification*, 32.

> Forgive for Christ's sake, my doubts about your goodness. Teach me to love your will more than my life. By Christ I ask this, Amen.

Selfishness claims that you can do the best for you.

You believe you know the best. By yourself you believe you can create the means to the best. You believe you have the power to be the best for yourself. Selfishness promises and delivers calamity, chaos, and curse.

But God identifies himself with your welfare. Remember the first words of the Sermon on the Mount (Matthew 5–7): "Blessed are …." God said, "I will bless you …."[13]

Selfishness breaks covenant with God.

Covenant is a two-party contract. God and people are the parties in the agreement. But people always sever the covenant bond and pledge.

God alone is faithful to his covenant obligations.

Selfishness negates the grace of God.

Selfishness operates for the good of my self and the glory of man. The sinful self chooses whatever is deemed right by the person. Every aspect of those choices is opposed to the grace and redemption of God.

Grace is always sufficient, pride-killing, and God-exalting. Grace acts for the good of another and the glory of God.

Selfishness is unbelief.

Selfishness is confused. It values what is passing away, and it derogates the eternal. People give their lives every day for their pleasures,

---

[13] Cf. Genesis 12:2; Haggai 2:19; and Hebrews 6:14. The believer blesses God in return in Psalms 63:4 and 145:2.

and they deny and obscure the eternal in their thinking, willing, and feeling. They justify their actions by what is "wrongly called knowledge" (1 Timothy 6:20). They argue with and deny the truth of God.

> ... because they exchanged the truth about God for a lie and worshiped and served the creature rather than the Creator, who is blessed forever! Amen. (Romans 1:25)

Selfishness avoids self-examination except in the most superficial and congratulatory manner.

The self says, "I deserve," "I did it," or "I am good." God's Word says, "All have sinned and fall short of the glory of God" (Romans 3:23).

Selfishness denies God as the giver of every good and perfect gift.

The selfish don't believe God is good (cp. 2 Chronicles 5:13, 7:13; Psalm 100:4–5, 106:1, 118:1, 136:1, 145:9, 15, 16; Jeremiah 33:11; and Acts 14:17).[14]

How different is the call of God's Word: "Give thanks to the Lord, for he is good."(Psalm 107:1).

Selfishness presumes upon the patience of God.

The selfish believe that God's severity against sin is not going to be executed immediately. Presuming God will not act against you is a very dangerous way to live.

God is slow in his wrath.[15] God is gracious and forbearing with people.

> He who is often reproved, yet stiffens his neck, will suddenly be broken beyond healing. (Proverbs 29:1)

---

14 Packer, *Knowing God*, 147.
15 Edwards, *Charity and Its Fruits*, 228; and Packer, *Knowing God*, 149. Cf. Nehemiah 9:17; Psalm 103:8, 145:8; Joel 2:13; and Jonah 4:2.

Suffering with Christ

The dichotomies and divisions of the self are clarified when you suffer. When you suffer, the Dark Guest is quelled:

> Since therefore Christ suffered in the flesh, arm yourselves with the same way of thinking, for whoever has suffered in the flesh has ceased from sin. (1 Peter 4:1)

Suffering ought not to be feared, but celebrated.

> Then they left the presence of the council, rejoicing that they were counted worthy to suffer dishonor for the name [of Jesus]." (Acts 5:41)

Toward the end of his ministry, Paul appears to have gained a new freedom from the appeals of men by his yielded obedience to God's will and his willingness—even eagerness—to faithfully stand trial and suffer for his faith. Though he was warned by the prophet Agabus not to go to Rome, Paul was driven by his desire to suffer before Nero for the name of Christ (cf. Acts 21:10–14). He knew that suffering was God's will for him, and though it would be extraordinarily difficult, he welcomed it.

Paul seemed compelled to go to Rome and to suffer for his faith. He was not like John Mark, who perceived a growing danger from the opponents of the Gospel and ran away just when the journey became dangerous (Acts 13:13). John Mark ran home just before Paul was stoned at Lystra (Acts 14:19). When Paul was told that he would suffer in Rome, he chose it. He ran to Rome that he might suffer for the Gospel and die. Suffering for the name of Jesus Christ is to bear in our bodies the marks of Jesus:

> From now on let no one cause me trouble, for I bear on my body the marks of Jesus. (Galatians 6:17)

You must choose either suffering or selfishness. They are the only options you have as a believer in Christ. The choice is real and the results in your life are categorical. Suffering would never be chosen by a person who is self-preserving. But suffering may be the clearest identifying mark of those who follow Christ. The decision to suffer and die for one's faith has been preferred to life by many thousands of believers because the Gospel of Christ is more valuable than life (cf. Psalm 63:3; Matthew 18:8–9). You may not be called upon to shed blood for your faith. But should not all true believers in Christ be willing to do so? What can man do to you?

> So we can confidently say, "The Lord is my helper;
> I will not fear; what can man do to me?" (Hebrews 13:6)

Resolutions

1. To become obedient to God from the heart, freely choosing my sanctification.
2. To own my own crucifixion (representatively), to die to self and to live for God.
3. To take up my cross daily, following Christ in his sufferings, living like Christ lived, and dying as Christ died.
4. To choose God's will for my life as the best for me.
5. To practice continual confession: If I am immoral, I must come to Christ with that sin; if I am immature in my faith, I must bring him my unlearned heart; if I am rebellious, if I fall short of God's standards, or twist some gift of God, I must repent.
6. To hide nothing in my life from God.
7. To know that every sin in my life can be defeated by Jesus Christ my Savior; no sin can hold me captive; victory is mine by Christ alone.
8. To grow in my hatred of sin.
9. To practice the duty and freedom of walking in newness of life, the fullness of the Holy Spirit, and the power of the resurrection.
10. To be flooded with the love of God.
11. To be on guard against any inclination of my heart that would doubt the love of God for me.
12. Like Paul, to come to suffer.

Chapter Four

The Triggers of Desire

We believe in the Inferno ... because we have trudged on our own two feet from end to end of it.[1]

... the act of will consenting to evil.[2]

A Christian can consent to evil. It happens all the time. You know people who consented to evil. You have probably joined in on the party yourself. You have become familiar with the territory of sin. You have watched something on TV or read something that corrupted your mind and heart for a long time. Or worse, you have been enticed, betrayed, and imprisoned by your sin. One of the greatest disappointments I experienced as a young Christian (in the late 1960s) was to learn that older believers I had deeply respected had committed some really horrible sins. Later, I knew that I was capable of their sins and much worse. Something was wrong with me.

Something is wrong with you, too. You are vulnerable to fall under sin's power. Temptations not only come into your life from spiritual forces and from other people but also from within you.

You are influenced by sin because you like it. Sin may be extremely enjoyable for a while. A spirit of independence and excitement comes from doing what you want. Oh, it takes you to Hell in a bus, but you don't think about that while the fun is on.

---

1   Sayers, *Further Papers on Dante*, Vol. 2, 10.
2   Sayers, *Introductory Papers*, Vol. 1, 133.

Your sin nature knows your vulnerabilities. It understands what you want and how you want it served. It gives you what you desire. If you spoke the truth about your desires to most of your friends they would be shocked, disgusted, and disappointed in you. The bad news is they have their own secrets too.

The Christian who is living under the power of the Dark Guest is double-minded, double-willed, and double-hearted. He is torn between two categorically different loves. He is assured and ashamed at the same time. He says he wants to live a holy life, but when he fails to do so, he presumes upon God's grace and forgiveness, and never progresses beyond the pattern of making messes of his life and then asking God to clean up after him.

The triggers of desire infect your thinking, choices, and emotions. Most sins are caused by one or more of these three triggers. If you know where the battles will be, you can have a good defense to keep the enemy out and maintain a strong offense to win the war.

Lust, greed, and pride

A trigger is a point at which sin makes entry into your life. It may be a point of vulnerability or emotional need forging an almost unbreakable connection to some destructive or damning choice, as in addictions to drugs, sex, control, or fame. A trigger often works on deeply felt needs for significance or safety, and then it shames and maims you.

Lust, greed, and pride are the triggers the Dark Guest uses to destroy your Christian life and to make your life a living hell.

These triggers set in motion actions, words, and choices that are not good for you. You know deep inside they are wrong and that they are not God's will for you. You will be disobeying God when you follow your desires. But you find yourself caught up in the moment, carried along by the rush. You push caution to the wind and are caught up in a tornado of desire that only increases the pain of life.

Many otherwise good and respectable people have had a

particularly horrid sin triggered by some deep desire within them. Their trysts made the evening news or national newspapers. Did they not think they would get caught? Did they not think about how it would be to read about their sin in the newspaper? See it on TV news? Pull it up on a web blog? In an early scene in Dante's *Inferno* (Canto 3, 51–55), people push one another out of the way, rushing to get on the boat crossing the river Acheron going to Hell. First Charles Williams comments:

> All the crowd of souls who wait on the bank [of the River awaiting the boat to take them to Hell] are those who have willingly insisted on the necessity of their own wishes. They now blaspheme. The whole multitude of souls, "weary and naked" thronging there, throw themselves into the boat, 'one by one'...."Why so hasty to pass?" Their fear is changed to a horrid desire of that which remains hateful; this is their finality.
>
> "No good ever passes here," never experiences this infernal conflict. The good have passed that conflict long since, once perhaps they disliked what they desired, but they gave themselves to that Order and Necessity which these others here blaspheme; ....[3]

Now Dorothy Sayers writes:

> All their fear is turned into desire.[4]

---

3   Williams, *The Figure of Beatrice*, 115–116. This scene is similar to the scene at the end of Purgatory (Canto 33, 127, p. 334) with a greatly different result. Dante comes to cross the River Eunoë ("good remembrance") where forgiveness does its work on the memory of all past sins; cf. Sayers in Dante, *Purgatory*, 335 and 339.
4   Sayers, *Introductory Papers*, Vol. 1, 133.

Romans 7 and desire

> What then shall we say? That the law is sin? By no means! Yet if it had not been for the law, I would not have known sin. For I would not have known what it is to covet if the law had not said, "You shall not covet." (Romans 7:7)

Paul's conflict with the power and personal presence of indwelling sin helps you understand your personal war within. Romans 7:7 is a reference to Exodus 20:17 and Deuteronomy 5:21. Paul is quoting a portion of the 10th Commandment. He wrote a truncated version of the commandment: "You shall not *desire*" (ESV reads "covet"). He omitted the objects of the verb—"your neighbor's house," etc. Because the object is left out, Paul was saying that it is not what is desired that is under consideration, but the *act of desire* itself.

We use "desire" in several different ways in modern English.[5] Some desires are very good. You desire that your kids be healthy. You desire a happy marriage. But Paul's use of desire is about the passions, the lusts, the sin-driven longings of the heart. C.K. Barrett lays out the meaning of Paul in Romans 7:

> Desire means precisely that exaltation of the *ego* which we have seen to be the essence of sin .... Regardless of his place in creation, and of God's command, man desires, and his desire becomes the law of his being. He, rather than God, becomes Lord. This the law cannot tolerate. Its form is God's command, and its basis is God's right as Lord to command. It emphasizes man's creatureliness. Its

---

5   The range is from "something you want," on one point of the compass, all the way to the "Desire of Nations" referring to Christ in Haggai 2:7 (KJV). The ESV translates the phrase in Haggai: "the treasures of all nations."

> fundamental requirement, illustrated in a great variety of particular precepts and prohibitions, might be summed up in two clauses: Thou shalt not desire—Thou shalt obey; and if both are left without objects their meaning becomes not less but more clear. The inexactness of Paul's quotation is not due to carelessness or to the wish to abbreviate, but contributes significantly to his own meaning, and to the understanding of the commandment that he quotes.[6]

The ego's *desire* for self-exaltation is always associated with denying the Lord and disobeying his holy law. Further, to be in submission to God and to live under the Lordship of Christ is expressed through a new *desire* to do only what God wishes. This is clearly heard in Christ's prayer in the Garden, "Not my will, but yours be done." (Luke 22:42). Christ *desired* the will of his Father more than life—more than anything.

Contrast the fact that the *desires* are the center zone of the sinful self to openly demonstrate its yearnings to resist God's will, to disobey, to rebel against his pure and holy purposes, to turn away from his wise counsel, to twist good gifts into our delights, and to subvert God's rule over our lives. Sin takes action. Sin defeats the Apostle. It is sin that perverts the law of God. That is why Paul can write that he "knows sin" (Romans 7:6). You know sin, too.

Pulling the trigger

The trigger of *desire* sets in motion a world of evil in the human heart. Notice that it is not the law that causes the trigger to be pulled. It is sin. "Sin seized its opportunity through the commandment." The trigger was activated because the law highlighted sin. Tell a child, "Don't touch the cookies!" and the kid will have a cookie in

---

6   Barrett, *The Epistle to the Romans*, 132.

his hands in a flash.

The commandment teaches us about the nature and operation of sin. Yet our desires take information that ought to be used to warn us of the terrible consequences, the punishment, and the fruit of our actions and, instead, plant the motivation for us to do the very thing that was forbidden by the law.

Sayers saw in Dante that the damned are deeply attached to their sin. They chose sin not because it was good, or because the consequences were desirable:

> They hate what they chose, yet because they chose it they cling to it.[7]

Sin always enslaves. Chamblin writes:

> Slavery to sin is bondage to self.[8]

But the slave clings to what enslaved him. People experience the consequences of sin—horrible afflictions, the loss of precious friend-ships, loves, possessions, and position—yet they persist:

> The iniquities of the wicked ensnare him, and he is held fast in the cords of his sin. He dies for lack of discipline, and because of his great folly he is led away. (Proverbs 5:22–23)

> Their deeds do not permit them to return to their God. For the spirit of whoredom is within them and they do not know the LORD. (Hosea 5:4)

Nothing is more pathetic than a person who continues to choose actions that destroy his life. Some people cling to insatiable desires,

---

7 Sayers, *Introductory Papers*, Vol. 1, 133.
8 Chamblin, *Paul and the Self*, 49–51.

chronic sins, and perpetual habits of soul and body. Their deeds alone alienate them from people, from success in their endeavors, and from God. Because these choices are their choices, they are unassailable. Try talking an adulterer out of his adultery. Try convincing a lazy man that hard work is what he needs. Try changing the heart of a man addicted to internet porn. Just because you know there is a speed limit doesn't make you want to go 30 in a residential area. The law means nothing to a law-breaker.

Religious people (not necessarily Christian) who are placed under the tutelage of God's law may become *worse* lawbreakers than those who are ignorant of the law's demands. *Desire* ignites sin by means of the law.

Then how should the law be taught? Do you teach the law as a guide to living? Do you encourage people to obey the law of God? Do you challenge people to be law-keepers? After all, doesn't Paul say that the law is good?

> So the law is holy, and the commandment is holy and righteous and good. (Romans 7:12)

The law is good, but the law isn't the problem. The struggle comes not because of the law, but because of indwelling sin. The Dark Guest finds in the law a way to make sin "sinful beyond measure" (Romans 7:13). Trying to obey the law will crush you. Using the law as a guide to life will create more sin in you than if you had avoided the law. It would be disastrous for you to negotiate with God on the basis of your law-keeping. As much as you would like to try to make yourself better, the Dark Guest cannot be sanctified. It needs to be put to death.

> ... yet we know that a person is not justified by works of the law but through faith in Jesus Christ, so we also have believed in Christ Jesus, in order to be justified by faith in Christ and not by works of the law, because by works of the law no one will be justified. (Galatians 2:16)

Applying Romans 7

Can a Christian keep the law of God? Yes, but only through faith in Christ, and only by the Holy Spirit. Trying to keep the law by yourself will crush you. Many Christians are taught to obey God by following the law, and it always destroys them. They cannot be good enough; they cannot be free from desires. They acknowledge that the law is good, and it kills them. The law cannot sanctify. It can only condemn.

Does this not explain why so many Christians are seen as hypocrites by the world? They proclaim their adherence to the law of God and always fail to keep it. Does this not explain why so many Christian leaders have been destroyed by their *desires*? They thought their office would make them obedient to God's law and they stopped waging war on sin.

You must be warned about the power of indwelling sin that continues to work within you through your desires. Here is a mirror to hold up to your heart; a little study on desire. Reading through these verses there should be little doubt about the war you wage against sinful desires:

> For the wicked boasts of the desires of his soul, and the one greedy for gain curses and renounces the Lord. (Psalm 10:3)

> Grant not, O Lord, the desires of the wicked; do not further their evil plot, or they will be exalted! (Psalm 140:8)

> ... but the cares of the world and the deceitfulness of riches and the desires for other things enter in and choke the word, and it proves unfruitful. (Mark 4:19)

> You are of your father the devil, and your will is to do your father's desires .... (John 8:44)

But put on the Lord Jesus Christ, and make no provision of the flesh, to gratify its desires. (Romans 13:14)

For the desires of the flesh are against the Spirit, and the desires of the Spirit are against the flesh, for these are opposed to each other, to keep you from doing the things you want to do. (Galatians 5:17)

And those who belong to Christ Jesus have crucified the flesh with its passions and desires. (Galatians 5:24)

... to put off your old self, which belongs to your former manner of life and is corrupt through deceitful desires. (Ephesians 4:22)

... knowing this first of all, that scoffers will come in the last days with scoffing, following their own sinful desires. (2 Peter 3:3)

These are grumblers, malcontents, following their own sinful desires; they are loud-mouthed boasters, showing favoritism to gain advantage. (Jude 16)

Your Word is always true, Gracious Lord, but my desires have pulled my eyes from your face, they have clouded my memory of your commands with such longings for what you have forbidden, that I cannot hear your warnings.

I have lied to myself about my desires. I have tolerated my sin within me, and have excused my disobedience to your Law. I have presented myself as a good person, but you know the truth about my passions. My daydreaming is not about your glory or perfections; it is about my happiness and success, my fulfillment and independence from you.

O God! I have imagined myself exalted, embraced, and delighted by what you have declared to be full of vanity, lust, and godlessness. I have, in my sin, the ability to call myself a Christian, yet still grieve your Spirit and disobey your Word. By selfishness and pleasures I disavow your love for me. How can I survive being so torn between what is so wonderful and good and by what is so hateful and onerous to your heart?

Could I desire only you, Redeemer God? Could I be compelled only to please you? To love only you? To choose only what you permit? To hate what you hate? Lord Jesus, please, I beg you, my desires that break your heart, utterly crush them.

My sin-filled desires permeate every choice I make. Once they are established in me, I am lost. O God, deliver me from my desires for what you have condemned. By my Christ's redeeming love I ask, Amen.

Triggers of lust, greed, and pride

The triggers of desire touch every Christian's life with a powerful trinity that work to defeat holiness in you. When you know where the war is fought, you can defend your heart. 1 John 2:15–16 crystallizes the desires into a horrid trinity of lust, greed, and pride:

> Do not love the world or the things in the world. If anyone loves the world, the love of the Father is not in him. For all that is in the world—the desires of the flesh and the desires of the eyes and pride in possessions—is not from the Father but is from the world. (1 John 2:15–16)

1 John 2:15-16 ties this horrid trinity to the world. The triggers are parts of the world system. Love the world and you are playing with the triggers of desire that can destroy you. Desire comes from deep within the human heart. *Lust* is played out in the chaos you create by illicitly gratifying your sexual needs. *Greed* is expressed by longing for financial security or success and the resentment that builds in you over people who succeed more than you, or who hinder your aspirations for wealth. Overarching *pride* in accomplishment, standing, influence, or power, chronicle most of human history, the drama of your neighbors, or the exploits of your teenagers. The names and events will change, but the plots will be similar in character. Without rehearsing, you could be starring in a soap opera.

The greatest people have held these faults in check. The worst of humanity has given expression to them. Reasonable people understand that unfettered lust is damaging to love and ruinous to true intimacy. One need not be a believer in Christ to observe the destruction caused by unchecked human lust to conclude that it is oppositional to true love.

Human wickedness needs no commentary, only billions of apologies. Too much of it is paraded before you on the evening news or experienced directly in your own legacy of broken relationships. Do you not grieve that sin has wasted so much potential, so much which could have been accomplished, except for the fact that people don't get along?

Few rules guide how these severing siblings of lust, pride, and greed work themselves out in human lives. Some may struggle with one and only one of them. Others will fight a dancing ring of temptation in which two or three of these powerful enemies work together to break a believer's connections to God and to tie him to the world. Love, peace, trust, kindness, and beauty are the casualties in this warfare. One person's sinful pleasure is another's spiritual pride.

One person may be tormented with longings for, say, a Ferrari. Another suffers from greed (same sin as the Ferrari guy), but he hordes his wealth and helps no one but himself. He drives an old Honda instead of the Italian sports car because he is so stingy with his money. Charles Williams writes:

> The misers and spendthrifts are seen everlastingly butting great stones against each other; the one side shriek: 'Why hoard?' the other: 'Why squander?' It is no wonder that the guardian of this circle [of Hell] is Plutus—the ancient god of wealth, a bloated figure clucking out meaningless sounds. All Hell repeats itself; this is futility again, but a futility more hateful because more full of hate.[9]

If you understand these triggers, you can see them all around you. Triggers make their corroding appeal at every turn in our modern culture. They are regular guest stars on TV soap operas, reality shows, the dramas of young women gone wild, the rise and fall of the famous, and even the mini dramas unfolding in your own neighborhood. Politics is filled with the self-absorbed, the arrogant, and the deceived. Churches and Christian missions and ministries give plenty of examples of what *not* to do for Jesus.

This isn't new. Shakespeare is famous because his plays explore the desires of the human heart. His plays, even the comedies, strike a note of truth about the selfishness of people. You read Shakespeare's *Julius Caesar* and you recognize something in him, pathetic as he

---

9   Williams, 121; cf. Dante, *Hell*, trans. Sayers, Canto 6, 9, p. 104; and Canto 7, 58–62, pp. 111–112.

was, that is all too familiar, even personal. People lie, they betray, and hate. Some people create lives in which they are terribly alone. People fail, they fall foolishly, stupidly in love, and then people die. You get it.

In fact, much of great literature won a following because it so accurately mirrors the nature of humanity's frailties to the readers. Their stories resonate with the truth about people and their sins. Whether it is Shakespeare's plays about *King Lear*, or *Macbeth*, or the terrifying kids in William Golding's *The Lord of the Flies*, or the cartoon characters on *The Simpsons*, you are drawn to these stories because they are true to the human condition, not because they are uplifting. Many of them are humorous, but some are quite disturbing. The deeds of human sin are the main subjects of popular literature because people, with a macabre interest, love their sinful desires.

Look for the triggers of desire in the pages of Scripture, and King David immediately jumps off the page as an embarrassingly detailed example of how not to live. David fell into adultery with Bathsheba because of his lust. But that may not have been all that was at work in his heart. Pride certainly was there as well. He didn't want to be discovered, so David had his lover's husband placed at the front of the battle so he would be killed.

However, it was not only lust and pride that moved him. There was within him a horrid greed to have another man's wife. Pride moved him to lie to the prophet of God about what he had done. David was famous for the lust, but lost his family and suffered for the rest of his life because of greed and pride (cf. 2 Samuel 11 and 12, through the end of 2 Samuel).

Judah's fall with Tamar in Genesis 38 is one more disgusting example. Judah slept with a prostitute, who became pregnant with his child. She was his daughter-in-law in disguise. She is brought to him without the disguise three months later, when she is accused of immorality. She reveals his part in her pregnancy and he repents (to a point) and confesses his role. It reads like a racy novel. Stories like this in the Bible ring true because we know people like this. The Bible records what the human heart does and is capable of. The report isn't pretty. These stories leave you disappointed and disgusted.

The list of Bible characters that failed and fell is too long to put here but it is worth study. Most of the characters in the Bible stumble somehow. Be warned. You can learn about yourself from the cautionary accounts of the leaders of Israel in the Bible. They were important people. They were people like you doing things you can imagine doing. If you read the Bible, you may sin less.

O Lord, you know and you see everything I have done. How thankful I am that my sins are not written down in your Book for others to read. Remind me of the truth that no sin recorded in Scripture is too repugnant for my broken self to commit. Forbid that I may never congratulate myself about the sins I didn't commit, because as you know too well, I only failed to sin more because I had been spared the opportunity.

Your Book reads my heart. It illuminates my inward filth. It labels my sin as sin, not as a mistake, a misunderstanding, or a character flaw. Before your face, Dear Lord, I can take responsibility for my own sin. I did it because I wanted it. And my heart breaks with sorrow over what I have done or could have done. You have limited my wandering to darker places by the fences and gates of your Providence. Left to myself, I would have done much worse.

I grieve how I have sinned before your watching eyes. Forgive me for forgetting David and Judah; for forgetting my huge sins and remembering only my small obediences. I am a hypocrite and a sinner. Others are more righteous than I.

Teach me holiness and love of God in the place of my Judah-like impurities and lies, and my David-like lust, pride, and greed. By Jesus Christ alone I ask. Amen.

---

1 The Lust of the Flesh:

The phrase "of the flesh" means that lust is empowered by the sin nature. The sin nature is called the "flesh." Any of the cravings of the sinful self can deteriorate into an enslaving lust.

Lust can dwell outside the realm of the prurient. What about beautiful colors or music? Robert Candlish writes about some less obvious candidates for lust:

> ... the eye for beauty and the ear of the soul for music ...
> But they all, every one of them, may become the lust of the flesh.[10]

A game that gives exercise and emotional release to one person can become a god before whose altar daily offerings are laid to another. I heard about an ex-pro golfer who held up a golf ball while giving his testimony during a church service. He pointed to it and said, "This was my god!" Lots of Christians play golf without becoming idolaters. He couldn't.

The most common trial brought into people's lives by the lust of the flesh is in the matter of sexual fidelity and purity. How quickly God's good gift of marital sex can be used for completely different ends than God intended. How terrible when a good gift of God can be twisted into an enslaving addiction that bears no resemblance to the gift or the Giver. Fidelity and chastity matter to God, and they should matter to every believer.

If one became aware of the lust of the flesh as a trigger, walls of protection would be constructed to bar the soul from falling into so

---

10 Candlish, *A Commentary of 1 John*, 145.

deep a snare. If one were waging a war against sexual sin, wisdom would suggest eliminating opportunities and exercising continual diligence in accountability to live according to God's design. Lust, in its many forms, can be a powerful and overwhelming enemy.

2 The Lust of the Eyes (Greed):

Desire is tied to what you think about. This is the desire that comes from your contemplation. Greed can be stirred up by thinking about the object of lust.[11]

This lust appears when your neighbor gets something that you had been longing for. If he buys a toy you wanted, your desire for the item is ignited into a flame of passion.

Have you ever made a spontaneous purchase and later regretted it? Your thinking is no barrier to your stupidly buying something you didn't need or couldn't afford. You see something you *really* want and then whip out the Visa® and *slam, bam,* it's yours. Thinking doesn't restrain greed. You can justify any purchase with logic (a form of thinking) when greed is pushing the shopping cart.

Seeing your neighbor gain what you desire, your heart is inflamed. It is about being jealous when he gets what *you* want. It isn't just a desire to have for yourself. Greed demands that your neighbor *not* have what you long for. You say in your heart, "How could he get *and enjoy* what I want?"

Greed grows when it watches others being happy or enjoying the good gifts of God in their daily lives. Greed occurs when a colleague or co-worker gains success in your company when you were passed by. When greed strikes, you resent his happiness, despise his success, and deride his abilities so that you feel better.

Greed requires a great love of this world. If you didn't love the world, you wouldn't care two wits whether anyone got more stuff or more success or more *whatever* he got. Why do you care?

The world has beautiful and enticing rewards for her friends. It offers beautiful homes, beautiful people, incredible cars, diamonds,

---

11 Ibid., 147.

gold, and status. Many people spend their lives in pursuit of these rewards. And they will all die broke and ugly.

You may long for a title for yourself and bitterly resent that recognition for others. Don't let him get his fancy title before you get yours, or you will hate him! People are ridiculous! What title does God have? King of kings. Lord of lords.

Greed is measured by what you have, what others have, and how you desire to control the difference between the two.

3 The Boastful Pride of Life:

The pride of life is our *boasting* derived from the things of this world, rather than from the life you have with God. Candlish writes:

> The vainglory which springs out of and belongs to our visible earthly life.[12]

> You are free, as to both of these instruments [lust of the eyes and the lust of the flesh] of the world's power. But what of its opinion? Have you learned to defy it, or to be independent of it? Can you dispense with the world's approval and brave its frown? Do you not sometimes find yourselves more afraid or ashamed of a breach of worldly etiquette,—some apparent descent from the customary platform of worldly respectability,—than of such a concession to the world's forms and fashions as may compromise your integrity in the sight of God, and your right to acquit yourselves of guile? The opinion of the world! What the world will think or say![13]

---

12 Westcott, *The Epistles of St. John*, 65.
13 Candlish, *A Commentary of 1 John*, 149.

The opinion of the world means far too much to your sinful self. The world needs to be put in its place. Sayers writes about the falsifiers (lustful, greedy, and prideful in the 10th Ditch of *The Inferno*). They cause such loss, but still they persist in wreaking havoc:

> Every value is false; it alternates between deadly lethargy and a raving insanity. All intercourse is corrupted, every affirmation becomes perjury, and every identity a lie ... (the) general bond of love and nature is utterly dissolved.[14]

Contrast the promise of the Word of God:

> And the world is passing away along with its desires, but whoever does the will of God abides forever. (1 John 2:17)

Triggers, an operational manual

Lust, greed, and pride are vicious enemies that empower your sinful nature to suggest terrible sins that are unimaginable for a holy person to commit. Yet you do commit them because sin still influences your life. You do what you hate! John Owen speculates that unredeemed men could be much worse than they are:

> And the reason why a natural man is not perpetually in the pursuit of some one lust, night and day, is because he has many to serve, every one crying to be satisfied; thence he is carried on with great variety, but in general he lies toward the satisfaction of self.[15]

An unbeliever could be much worse than he is, but he doesn't

---

14 Sayers, *Introductory Papers*, Vol. 1, 146.
15 Owen, *Overcoming Sin and Temptation*, 73.

have the strength to chase all the sins he can imagine. As a believer in Christ, the Spirit of God works within you to restrain your sin to make you much better.

To wage war on your lusts you will need:

Awareness—You can operate by the power of the Spirit of God when you know how terribly weak you are against the triggers. To think of oneself as strong as you war against your lusts is insanity. It is wise to acknowledge you are vulnerable to the triggers and to understand where your particular weaknesses lay. You can build a defense against them by the fullness of the Holy Spirit, the Word of God, a daily walk with God, and friends who hold you accountable for living the Christian life.

Confession—You cannot live the Christian life by your own efforts. If you try, you will fail. Rather, acknowledge your desire to sin, your longings to give yourself to lust, pride, and greed, then seek with all your redeemed soul to confess them all.

Love for God—The believer is not just an obeyer of God. He is a lover of God. You love God with all your heart, soul, mind, and strength (cf. Deuteronomy 13:3; Luke 10:27). Loving God provides everything you need. Why would the world look so sweet to someone who loved God with all his heart? What could be more appealing than the pleasure of God? What could be more valuable than God's delight in you?

Get over the world.

Resolutions

1. To know I am capable of consenting to evil and that I sin because I love it.
2. To be assured of God's love and ashamed of my sin simultaneously.
3. To pray, strive, and choose against my sinful desires.
4. To confess that my sinful desires are rebellions against God's holy will for my life and are destructive of my holiness.
5. To know that the law of God will utterly crush me; that I cannot, on my own, keep any command of God, but that I am, in my flesh, a law breaker always and only.
6. To trust in Christ alone to fulfill the law of God within me, writing his law upon my heart, to form a new man within me who loves the law of God.
7. To be warned against my sinful desires that can destroy my faith, my witness, my loves, and my life.
8. To grieve how much potential for good my sinful heart has wasted.
9. To trust in Christ alone to save me from my sins, knowing that he protects my soul daily by his continual prayers on my behalf.

Chapter Five

Declaration of War

Take heed to yourselves also because there are many eyes upon you. So there will be many who observe your fall. If you miscarry, the world will also echo with it. It is the same as the eclipses of the sun in broad daylight—they are seldom without witnesses ... a great man cannot make a small sin.[1]

For if you live according to the flesh you will die, but if by the Spirit you put to death the deeds of the body, you will live. (Romans 8:14)

We are at a strange time in the history of Christianity. As in no other epoch, our current day has broken almost completely from the way earlier followers of Christ lived their lives, served God, thought about themselves as those who will give account to God, worshiped God, sacrificed for the kingdom of God, and, most significantly, thought about God.[2]

---

1 Baxter, *Watch Your Walk (The Reformed Pastor)*, 70.
2 The time of the Reformation in the early 16th century may parallel to some extent the vacuity of today. Luther rediscovered Pauline theology, the biblical gospel, the glory of grace, and the power of the Word of God, all of which had been lost through the Middle Ages. Our sins are worse today because we have so much more testimony, so much greater a cloud of witnesses to bear testimony and to bring light to what the church has been entrusted. "For our appeal does not spring from error or impurity or any attempt to deceive, but just as we have been approved by God to be entrusted

No singing in Hell

The historical facts of the Christian faith—the life, death, and resurrection of Christ, his miracles and sovereign power over creation, and his authority and wisdom—do not compel a change in the character, passions, and will of the believer. Those events are compelling only after one has committed in love to the God who accomplished them. Before that commitment, they are facts that tell us more about sin than about God, because knowing *about* God changes nothing in us. Facts about God are all around us. We don't love God more because the stars are amazing. Sin dims all evidences of God's glory poured out in the splendor of creation's order and complexity. Sin silences choruses of praise shouting the greatness of his wisdom and the depths of his mercy. There is no singing in Hell.

How could anyone live his life today as though God had *not* come to Earth in the God-Man Jesus Christ of Nazareth?[3] Despite that visitation done publicly and seen by thousands, millions live apart from Christ and are condemned by their sin.

This age has very nearly displaced the worship of the One True God as an external-to-us, living Being to whom you must give an account, for a vision of a God who is little more than a projection of a man drawn large. Worshiping God in man's image is to shrink God and therefore it is to worship man. Karl Barth said, "You cannot speak about God by shouting MAN loudly."[4]

But the modern church is increasingly shouting "MAN," as the vision of God is shrinking to man-sized proportions and God is

---

with the gospel, so we speak, not to please man, but to please God who tests our hearts." (1 Thessalonians 2:3–4). Certainly no one needs to discover grace as they did at the end of the Middle Ages. But today we need to define it much more carefully.

3   Cf. Carnell, *The Burden of Søren Kierkegaard*. 113, 133–134.
4   Wells, *God in the Wasteland*, 108. Wells reflects on Karl Barth's analysis of Schleiermacher. Wells concludes, "For all his brilliance, Schleiermacher ended up knowing only himself, not God."

taken captive for the purposes of man in order to meet the needs of man. All early Christian creeds condemn such small views of God and large views of man. Today false views of God and man are celebrated among huge churches. Their faulty teaching is marketed to millions of American Christians. People are trying to find in themselves the way to God.

A.W. Pink identifies our great mistake:

> The great mistake made by most of the Lord's people is in hoping to discover in themselves that which is to be found in Christ alone.[5]

Faith, in this strange day, is an action that you do that captures the blessings of Christ's death on the cross so you won't be punished for your sins. This false faith comes from inside you. You are the subject and the object of your faith. God is a spectator, benefactor, and redeemer, but there is little connection with God in this faith. Faith is like currency you spend to get what you want. It arises from within you and moves God to do something for you. That false faith is expressive of indwelling sin, not true salvation.

True faith is a gift of God to the undeserving. Faith comes from God. Saving faith comes from outside of you. Unbelieving man is "faithless." But some have this false faith and they sincerely believe that their false faith will appropriate what Christ has done for their life. Faith is not innate. It doesn't come from you.

> I have been crucified with Christ. It is no longer I who live, but Christ who lives in me. And the life I now live in the flesh I live by faith in the Son of God, who loved me and gave himself for me. (Galatians 2:20)

For by grace you have been saved through faith.

---

5   Pink, *The Doctrine of Sanctification*, 200; cp. Bridges, *The Discipline of Grace*, 101.

> And this is not your own doing; it is the gift of God, not a result of works, so that no one may boast. (Ephesians 2:8–9)
>
> ... so that Christ may dwell in your hearts through faith—that you, being rooted and grounded in love. (Ephesians 3:17)
>
> And without faith it is impossible to please him, for whoever would draw near to God must believe that he exists and that he rewards those who seek him. (Hebrews 11:6)
>
> But as for the cowardly, the faithless, the detestable, as for murderers, the sexually immoral, sorcerers, idolaters, and all liars, their portion will be in the lake that burns with fire and sulfur, which is the second death. (Revelation 21:8)
>
> Cp. Luke 7:50; Acts 15:9; Romans 1:5; 1 Timothy 6:12; and 1 John 5:4.

Christian warfare

The first Christians described their lives as a warfare: striving, fighting, putting on armor, being soldiers, and following commands (cf. 1 Corinthians 9:7; 2 Corinthians 10:3f.; Ephesians 6:12; Philippians 2:25; 1 Timothy 1:18, 6:12; 2 Timothy 2:3; and Philemon 1:2). They saw themselves fighting a battle to the death. While John Bunyan was imprisoned, he wrote about this fierce conflict with evil:

> Then Apollyon straddled quite over the whole breadth of the way, and said, I am void of fear in this matter; prepare thyself to die: For I swear by my infernal den thou shalt go no further: here will

I spill thy soul.[6]

The Word prepares us for this war:

> Only let your manner of life be worthy of the gospel of Christ, so that whether I come and see you or am absent, I may hear of you that you are standing firm in one spirit, with one mind striving side by side for the faith of the gospel, and not frightened in anything by your opponent. (Philippians 1:27–28)

> But since we belong to the day, let us be sober, having put on the breastplate of faith and love, and for a helmet the hope of salvation. (1 Thessalonians 5:8)

> This charge I entrust to you, Timothy, my child, in accordance with the prophecies previously made about you, that by them you may wage the good warfare. (1 Timothy 1:18)

> Fight the good fight of the faith. Take hold of the eternal life to which you were called and about which you made the good confession in the presence of many witnesses. (1 Timothy 6:12)

> I have fought the good fight, I have finished the race, I have kept the faith. (2 Timothy 4:7)

God, the church, and the self

Our culture has infected the church with a debilitating disease. In some churches the self is more important than God. In 1994, David Wells writes about this new place of the self in the today's church:

---

6 Bunyan, *Pilgrim's Progress*, 51.

Stripped of external connectedness and haunted within by anxiety, modern individuals drift in society like bits of cork on the ocean, moved about in ways beyond their understanding by deep and irresistible currents. Filled with dread, "dis-ease," and foreboding and unable to secure a foothold in any external reality, they take refuge in the one certain thing remaining—the self. This turn to the self as the source of mystery, of meaning, and of hope is the key to understanding the shape that much religion in America has taken today ... any religion based on the self must itself be disordered.[7]

... We have turned to a God that we can use rather than to a God we must obey; we have turned to a God who will fulfill our needs rather than to a God before whom we must surrender our rights to ourselves. He is a God *for* us, for our satisfaction—not because we have learned to think of him through Christ but because we have learned to think of him this way through the marketplace.

... Pride is also self-centeredness that is pursued, protected and given shape as an alternative to submission to God and to being God-centered. It is a preoccupation with self as the goal of life. It is self-absorption and self-love. Thus it was that Dante pictured the proud man in Hell bent over the weight of an enormous stone: The gaze of the proud will never leave the Earth.[8]

When worship is a performance, the exposition of the Word

---

7   Wells, *God in the Wasteland*, 91–92, 97.
8   Ibid., 112, 114.

Chapter Five: Declaration of War

of God a self-help seminar, praise to God given only by paid professionals, prayer offered only for ourselves, programs concocted to attract finances, virtues reduced to niceness and acceptance of any sin, and unqualified spiritual leaders conduct ministries for the unsanctified, the church ought to be embarrassed to call itself the Body of Christ under these conditions.

Not every church is filled with people who worship themselves. But many are. The self can hijack the worship of God by establishing a spoken concern for the lost that keeps the church's focus on salvation, and not the sanctification of those who are saved. People in such groups are often puffed up, and exhorted to continue in their fruitless exercises, when a more effective application of energy may result in fewer numbers, fewer financial resources, and conflict with those who are living for themselves.

A group of people can never be sanctified as a whole, but individuals can. Jesus said something about the one and the 99 (cf. Matthew 18:13). People can be lost together in great numbers. When the needs of the self are unchecked, churches are much more like clubs and bowling alleys than the Body of Jesus Christ that labors to bring the Kingdom of God to human hearts.

But let's be clear about this difficulty. Churches fail because of the people in them. They choose vapid programs, tolerate heinous immoralities, and create classes that leave participants as babes in their faith. This is done because we are selfish.

We don't want the pastor to be holy or our leaders to be consecrated in any way that might create conflict within us. We want to be congratulated for our faith, not called to account for wasting so much time and potential. It is easy to condemn churches that offend in public and horrific ways. But what they do, we all do. We want success. Even churches that do all they can to stay unsuccessful, unhealthy and small, do so because they want it. They succeed at being inconsequential. They pride themselves in being unmoved by numbers and nickels! Pride and selfishness destroy the local church.

That is why we need a war. We need more than a meeting, a study, a paper, a conference, or a retreat. We need a war.

Forgive us, Holy God. We have subtracted perfections from your holiness. We have torn it apart, redefining it as what we want it to be. We have changed everything about you so that your qualities become more like everything in us. This assault on your character was not an explicit plan, but it was what our hearts wanted as our selfishness is affronted by your holy nature.

King of Glory, we would sit on Heaven's throne if you were not occupying it. Forgive us for not only changing you into someone like us, but in our sinful plunder, seeking to change your church as well.

We have made worship about our happiness, truth about our success, love about what others think of us, and the Gospel as permission for you to forgive and save us.

O Jesus! We have tried to change you into our image! What horrid idolatry this is! What rebellion rests in our hearts to plot your overthrow!

We came to worship and left thinking only about ourselves. We came to praise and left critical of song, message, and offering. We came to hear and left with our ears stuffed full of men's thoughts and their pitiable egos.

Would you wage a holy war in our hearts to reclaim your righteous Rule and Kingship in our lives? Wage war on our hearts that we may be won to you and for you in everything. By Christ's grace we pray this. Amen.

The war for holiness

> ... but I see in my members another law waging war against the law of my mind and making me captive to the law of sin that dwells in my members. (Romans 7:23)

> For though we walk in the flesh, we are not waging war according to the flesh. (2 Corinthians 10:3)

You are engaged in a war. You are rotted in this war, not blown apart by it. You are corroded by a seemingly inconsequential decision made with a sigh during an unguarded moment. An unthinking decision leads you to an unholy relinquishing of loyalty and servanthood to God; or perhaps after a long struggle to be hope-filled, an acquiescence to despair fills the dark places of the soul with marauding shadows that steal your peace and rob you of any assurance that you are God's—for an hour or a day or a year, or God forbid, a decade.

The sin nature (the "flesh") wages war against the Christian. That power wears down your virtue so that purity and holiness become burdens too heavy for you to carry. Will you be faithful but left to stand alone, as Paul?:

> At my first defense no one came to stand by me, but all deserted me. May it not be charged against them! (2 Timothy 4:16)

The loneliness of holiness can create deep despair. The price you pay to be faithful seems impossibly high. "If it be possible, let this cup pass from me!" Jesus had no Dark Guest, no indwelling sin, but he was tempted as you are. Cf. Hebrews 4:15.

Your sinful heart argues with your mind so that you might think less of the promises, peace, comfort, presence, hope, truth, and victory of the Gospel of Jesus. Sin cups your eyes and ears, compelling you to see and hear only the painful, pointless, never-ending arc of sorrows.

If sin could sever you from your Savior by these relentless assaults, it might be possible that you would be lost (cf. Matthew 24:24). But it can't break the bond of love and redemption with Christ. The Saving One never stops praying for you (John 17:9; Hebrews 7:25). You are in the midst of the war, with your life in the balance. Your eternity is daily being won by your Savior's blood and his prayers for you.

So you fight. You wage war. You agonize (cp. Philippians 3:13). This does not involved sitting, resting, contemplating, being polite, learning more, passively being inspired, getting your needs met, or planning and writing reports.

This is a horrid war. The enemy can destroy you (cf. Luke 22:31). You dare not fight bare-skinned and unshielded. The enemy's blows will bruise and break you. He doesn't fight according to rules. The sinful self has no honor. And your sin-filled heart works within you to help your enemy harm you. Indwelling sin weakens your courage, strips you of resolve, lowers your defenses, and creates moral weakness in you. He throws immensely heavy burdens on your back while taking away your sword and shield, and whispering in your ears that the battle is already lost. The call to put on armor is a command to prepare you to do battle with a hateful, vicious enemy.

You *must* put on the armor of God (cf. Ephesians 6:11 and 13). It is time to take out the armor and strap it on. Put on the sword and buckle it on tight. Now draw it from the scabbard. Put on your helmet for battle. Engage the enemy.

Remember you have a Commander in this conflict. Waging a war alone is a formula for sure defeat. You need a Commander to guide your assaults, to position you where you are most useful, and to shore up those who are likewise engaged, but who are hurting and wounded, or who have ceased to receive your Commander's orders.

Sayers paraphrases a selection from *Purgatory* that illustrates the sufficiency of grace, the mighty harbinger of blessing in the battle. The grace character—Beatrice—is personified love, God's wisdom, Christ's presence, and the Word of God, all merged into one character. Beatrice spoke to Dante throughout his adventure on his quest to be purged of his sin. Dante was crushed when he yielded to his sin; his lust got the better of him. She sharply rebuked him. Sayers retells the story:

> "Once, in me, you saw and loved your true good. The image of it was taken away from you when I died—but you had seen, was there any mortal thing that should have drawn you to lust after it, once you had seen *that*? Are you a grown man that you behave like a child? Lift up your beard and look at me."
>
> [Dante] looks and cannot bear the sight and falls unconscious.[9]

Listen to the Commander's orders and follow them. Get to the battle and put your life on the line. Engage! This is a life and death, Heaven and Hell, struggle. Wage a war:

Deny yourself

Take up your cross

Put to death what is earthly in you

Put on the breastplate of faith

Be crucified with Christ

Be raised with him

Do not entangle yourself in worldly affairs

---

9 Sayers, *Introductory Papers on Dante*, Vol. 1, 96; and Dante, *Purgatory*, trans. Sayers, Canto 31, 34–46, 67–73, 88, pp. 316–317.

> Fight the good fight
>
> Be holy

Two fronts of our war

The battle is both external—against your spiritual enemies—and internal against indwelling sin. A multifront war is the strategist's greatest fear.

Your war is against the world, the flesh, and the Devil. Two of these are external. One is internal. If you gain victory over one, two more are waiting to kill you. If you gain victory over two, one remaining vile enemy can destroy you. You must wage a threefold war. You are to put to death your sinful nature, your old self and the actions that rise from your sinful desires:

> For if you live according to the flesh you will die, but if by the Spirit you put to death the deeds of the body, you will live. (Romans 8:13)

> Put to death therefore what is earthly in you: sexual immorality, impurity, passion, evil desire, and covetousness, which is idolatry. (Colossians 3:5)

> Do not lie to one another, seeing that you have put off the old self with its practices. (Colossians 3:9)

Robert Mounce writes:

> So what I am by nature is in constant conflict with what I aspire to be as a child of God in whom the Spirit of God dwells.[10]

---

10 Mounce, *Romans*, 170.

This conflict goes to the core of what it means to be a believer in Christ—a person who is delivered from the penalty and power of sin. This deliverance, this salvation, is tangible and substantive. You are redeemed from sin that you might be sanctified. When you are made holy by Jesus Christ, you sin less. The Spirit of God conforms you more and more into the image of Christ (cp. Romans 8:29; 1 Corinthians 2:16; 2 Corinthians 3:18; Ephesians 4:13; and Philippians 2:5). That is the new person he has made you. You are now redeemed by Christ's blood.

The Spirit enlivens your will so that you desire to do what God wants and to be conformed to the likeness of Christ. But the Spirit chooses not to *compel* you to become holy, but to *transform* you into the kind a person who will freely, aggressively choose this conflict. You will long to sin less. You will begin to take more seriously your discipleship, obedience, godliness, and holiness of life. The Spirit makes you that new person who wills to become more like Christ. The Spirit brings more and more grace into your life.

But this process is not automatic, nor is it as far-reaching as it should be in the lives of believers. Despite the presence of Christ, the gift of the Holy Spirit, the promises of God and the hope of victory, still this warfare is being lost by many. God will not coerce you into being holy.

Christians are living in a life-and-death battle for their souls every day of their lives. Millions of Christians today are falling into outrageous sins. Without doubt the worst plague in the church today is the sin of sexual immorality.[11] Sexual impurity is rampant in the church among leadership and laity alike. But that is only one sin of the flesh.

---

11 Evangelicals make up between 28 percent to 34 percent of the American population. Barna reports that 7 percent of Evangelicals espoused the view that having sexual relations with persons to whom they are not married is morally acceptable. If America has about 300 million people, using the lower number (28 percent) of Evangelicals would be 5.88 million of them who hold that view. See "The Barna Update," *The Barna Group* (November 3, 2003), http://www.barna.org.

The warnings of Scripture are broadly unheeded and willfully mocked by the religious of our day. Scripture warns that these sins have eternal consequences. God is keeping an account of your life:

> Or do you not know that the unrighteous will not inherit the kingdom of God? Do not be deceived: neither the sexually immoral, nor idolaters, nor adulterers, nor men who practice homosexuality, nor thieves, nor the greedy, nor drunkards, nor revilers, nor swindlers will inherit the kingdom of God. And such were some of you. But you were washed, you were sanctified, you were justified in the name of the Lord Jesus Christ and by the Spirit of our God. (1 Corinthians 6:9–11)

Lust, greed, and pride have destroyed the fruitfulness and effective service of thousands of pastors and Christian leaders. Purity, contentment, and humility among those who claim to be believers in Christ are rare qualities. Satan is sifting us like wheat (Luke 22:31).

Instead of falling into sin, soiling the Gospel, deriding God's sufficiency, or tainting the promises of God, Christians today need to engage in a war within them. The doctrine of the sinful heart gives you a reality-base from which to build your strategy.

The Scriptures give you ample information about your struggles. Because you have absolutely nothing to hide from God, you now honestly face every one of your failures. In this warfare, by the Spirit of God, you honestly confess and completely repent of your sins. You see yourself as God sees you. Transformed by the Spirit of God, you have an honest starting point for growth in grace unto holiness of life.

You begin this war as a sinner who has been redeemed, and you grow to become more and more like Jesus Christ, who is your Lord. And this warfare wages in your soul through the mediation and indwelling power of the Spirit of God, by grace, for God's glory, until the day you die, that you might be like him when he appears. You will be like Christ!

> Beloved, we are God's children now, and what we will be has not yet appeared; but we know that when he appears we shall be like him, because we shall see him as he is. (1 John 3:2)

None of this will happen unless you declare war on indwelling sin. If you are to be more like Jesus Christ, you must die to your sin.

Sanctification

The Christian life is utterly different from the life of the sinful self. The self-denying follower of Christ seeks to know and do the will of God. He lives a life that others can see is consistent with the commands of God and can be imitated by other believers. His obedience flows out of the powerful working of the Spirit of God within him. He continues to abide in the love of God. When he falls, he knows with certainty that Christ will restore him. The sin nature is being annihilated. This is sanctification by the Spirit. Dante sought that day when sin would be put in its place:

> For when the ill soul faces him, confession
> Pours out of it till nothing's left to tell;
> Whereon that connoisseur of a transgression
> Assigns it to its proper place in Hell ... [12]

Sanctification is *not* training, disciplining, teaching, coercing, begging, cleaning up, modifying, or in any other way improving the Dark Guest so that it may become more holy. Your sinful nature cannot be sanctified.

You can be disciplined, careful in speech, or do loving things

---

[12] Dante, *Hell*, trans. Sayers, Canto 5, 7–8, p. 98.

for others, but if you do these things through your sinful nature, you will become less holy, less effective, less truly loving, and less fruitful in your Christian life.

The Dark Guest can lead a church ministry, come to meetings on time, read great books, speak the Christian "dialect," and do thousands of good works, but it cannot be holy. The Dark Guest can superficially imitate Jesus Christ, but it cannot live like Jesus, love like Jesus, obey God's will like Jesus, or be holy as Jesus is holy.

Many religious people have never known a truly holy Christian person who is filled with the Spirit of God and laboring for Christ with tremendous results and unstoppable joy.

The Dark Guest lies to you about what God requires of you, as though holiness is something you can generate from within yourself. Christians fail at holiness because they try to create it out of their sin.

A Christian can identify a behavior or discipline he believes would be helpful for him, something to help him grow in his faith, or an activity he heard from others would be beneficial for him. He then applies diligence to train himself to perform that activity or discipline.

For example, you might decide having a daily devotional or quiet time with the Lord would be good thing. Others who walk with God talk about their devotions and personal worship as central to their relationship with God and a mark of a serious disciple. So you think it must be important.

But you employ the flesh to master this skill. The Dark Guest trains you to rise early in the morning, to read the Bible, and to pray. You imitate all of these outward actions that are precisely what a holy believer would do. But in this case, you employ your sinful nature to be the means by which holiness is attained, just as the Pharisees did.

You create the discipline and with earnest effort practice it day after day. You are meticulous about setting aside time, reading portions of the Bible, and praying for people. But because you are attempting to sanctify the Dark Guest, the result is spiritual disaster.

Instead of daily devotions leading you to know the Lord more intimately you become less connected with God and more proud of your accomplishments. You brag about your discipline and seek ways to congratulate or reward yourself because of your success at rising early and performing your Bible study and quiet time. But something is terribly wrong.

You read the Bible more to store up information than to be a means of knowing God more intimately. You can be disciplined, methodical in reading, and consistent in meeting your goals. But the Dark Guest blocks all true spiritual growth. It takes the very act of daily devotions (which is a wonderful habit for any Christian) and he rewards you with pride, an unteachable, critical spirit, favoritism, and lovelessness because you sought to make yourself holy.

You cannot sanctify your sinful self. The Dark Guest's plans will never result in true holiness. Under its control no real confession or repentance will occur. The sinful heart will take a godly discipline, time in prayer, the study of God's Word, sermons preached, service to others, and the worship of God, and make the believer more proud, less humble, more judgmental, less patient with others, and more liable to fail in his inner, hidden virtues.

The Christian who knows the Dark Guest will choose to have devotions to do war against its evil influence. He will begin the worship of God with true confession, honest self-emptying and earnest repentance. The sinful self will be acknowledged, and then killed. The Word of God will greatly humble the heart, and it also will bring amazing comfort and encouragement. Reading the Word will be done not to brag about how holy he is but so that he might actually walk with God, who is holy.

The sinful self has been dominating, directing, and coaching, in many Christians' spiritual lives. These Christians are often earnest and disciplined. They can be active in attendance and engaged in service to God, but something is very wrong. The selfish Christian measures all he does by how it makes him look and what others will think. Or in worse cases, he believes that God will be indebted to him because he did X, therefore, God owes him Y. He selfishly engages in the same activities as the godly and is outwardly much the same as they. The actions and accomplishments of the Dark Guest are hard to distinguish from the deeds of humble and holy believers in Christ. It is God who looks at the heart (1 Samuel 16:7).

The life directed by your sinful nature can look very much like the obedient, sanctifying Christian, except for one crucial issue: *Jesus*. Indwelling sin may talk about Jesus, but it doesn't love him. The sinful self might do things "for Jesus," but it will always change, subtract, or modify that service to be something very different from what God intended.

Prayer can be empowered by your sinful nature. The Dark Guest can lead in prayer; but that prayer will be more about your wants and needs, more about your power and position, more about the turn of words and phrases, or the exaltation of yourself, than about training the heart to love God above all.

True prayer creates a chastening of your love for God, correcting your heart's flaws and failures. It confesses and empties the self of presumption and pride. True prayer receives grace to love God more. It diminishes the self, empties the heart in an outpouring of love to God and for God, while standing unworthy in the presence of God, yet accepted before his glorious Throne for Christ's sake, while there overflowing with joy and glory.

Prayers coming from the sinful heart may use words about Jesus, but they are not spoken in the Spirit of Jesus, with his wisdom, light, hope, mercy, forbearance, grace, and love. Those prayers are about words and talk, not God's presence, faith in action and truth spoken in love. They don't ring true. They are phony and religious.

Spirit-forged prayer takes everything you know, all you have learned about grace, mercy, and peace; all that the Word teaches about God's character and holiness; and it guides you into every insight you have gained about your sin and every lesson from the pages of Scripture by which you beheld yourself as in a mirror; and there you knew your sin and there you found your Savior. Prayer takes all you are and all you know, and it translates them all into praise of your Savior Jesus Christ by real holiness in you expressed by an obedient life, and love for God and for people.

Humility

The meek wage a mighty war. They shall inherit the Earth. The meek win! The humble are better equipped to declare war than the proud. The humble know their need of grace. "Blessed are the meek" (Matthew 5:5, cf. Psalm 37:11). They accomplish more for God than the proud. They are more effective because God gives them grace. God opposes the proud (James 4:6; 1 Peter 5:5).

The proud are engaged in rivalry and conceit. They are familiar with filthiness and wickedness. They are full of boasting that comes from within them. "All these evil things come from within, and they defile a person."(Mark 7:23).

The meek receive grace from God. They count others more significant than themselves. They receive the Word of God. They demonstrate good works.

The greatest men and women of all time have been humble. Today we don't expect the humble to be great leaders. We have chosen the arrogant or the self-reliant over the godly and self-effacing, and this has cost our churches and nation inestimable loss. The humble can be much more effective leaders than the arrogant.[13]

Without humility one cannot gain wisdom. Humility is self-emptying. It is a virtue that opens the door for many other virtues. Without humility one will not grow in love for others. Humility is the beginning place for every enduring friendship. Humility in relationships with other Christians flows into our relationship with God.

> Do nothing from rivalry or conceit, but in humility count others more significant than yourselves. (Philippians 2:3)

---

13 Collins, *Good to Great*.

> To this end we always pray for you, that our God may make you worthy of his calling and may fulfill every resolve for good and every work of faith by his power, so that the name of our Lord Jesus may be glorified in you, and you in him, according to the grace of our God and the Lord Jesus Christ. (2 Thessalonians 2:11–12)

> Therefore put away all filthiness and rampant wickedness and receive with meekness the implanted word, which is able to save your souls. (James 1:21)

> Who is wise and understanding among you? By his good conduct let him show his works in the meekness of wisdom. (James 3:13)

> Likewise, you who are younger, be subject to the elders. Clothe yourselves, all of you, with humility toward one another, for "God opposes the proud but gives grace to the humble." Humble yourselves, therefore, under the mighty hand of God so that at the proper time he may exalt you. (1 Peter 5:5–6)

The Word of God your unfailing ally

There is no such thing as an effective, mature, fruitful Christian who does not meditate on the Word of God (cf. Psalms 1 and 119).

> This Book of the Law shall not depart from your mouth, but you shall meditate on it day and night, so that you may be careful to do according to all that is written in it. For then you will make your way prosperous, and then you will have good success. (Joshua 1:8)

Chapter Five: Declaration of War

> In him you also, when you heard the word of truth, the gospel of your salvation, and believed in him, were sealed with the promised Holy Spirit. (Ephesians 1:13)

> ... because of the hope laid up for you in heaven. Of this you have heard before in the word of the truth, the gospel. (Colossians 1:5)

> For everything created by God is good, and nothing is to be rejected if it is received with thanksgiving, for it is made holy by the Word of God and prayer. (1 Timothy 4:4–5)

> Do your best to present yourself to God as one approved, a worker who has no need to be ashamed, rightly handling the word of truth. (2 Timothy 2:15)

> Of his own will he brought us forth by the word of truth, that we should be a kind of firstfruits of his creatures. (James 1:18)

The Holy Spirit your greatest helper

The only way to victory over the sinful self is through the in-dwelling power and filling of the Holy Spirit in the life of the believer. Apart from the Spirit, you can do nothing.

> For if you live according to the flesh you will die, but if by the Spirit you put to death the deeds of the body, you will live. (Romans 8:13)

> But I say, walk by the Spirit, and you will not gratify the desires of the flesh. (Galatians 5:16)

> If we live by the Spirit, let us also walk by the Spirit. (Galatians 5:25)

Dying to self is a brutal, messy business. There are no short cuts. But you have a Sovereign God who has given you his Holy Spirit. Out of your new heart, Christ is calling you to be a new person, a new creation.

Your indwelling sin cannot stand against the redemption of Christ. Sin has no power against the indwelling Spirit of God. It cannot influence you over the Word of God that is applied to your hearts by the Spirit of God. The Spirit of God applies the redemption of Christ to your life by changing your affections and shaping your loves. He gives you a heart of flesh, a soft heart that is alive and that beats in time with the heart of God.

A Christian becomes like Christ in character and heart (cf. Matthew 7:16, 20). You don't accept Christ merely to give him *permission* to forgive you. You believe "into" him. You believe in him—are born again—and are made new that you might glorify him in everything you think, choose, say, do, and feel. The promise of Heaven comes to you because your life is hidden with Christ in God. Heaven is where God is and you are adopted into God's family.

You decide to follow because he calls you and leads you by his Word and his Holy Spirit. You live for Christ because he lives in you. You love God because he first loved you. Your heart now flows with rivers of living water. Your selfish soul will drown in such a deep and life-giving flood:

> For out of the heart come evil thoughts, murder, adultery, sexual immorality, theft, false witness, slander. (Matthew 15:19)

> ... whoever believes in me, as the Scripture has said, "Out of his heart will flow rivers of living water." (John 7:38)

Heavenly King, empty me of my selfish longings. Your Word is so clear that my pride must die and my humility must grow if I am to become more like Jesus Christ.

Dear Savior, I do not even understand how to offer myself to you in humility of heart and in submission to your will. So much in me competes with your nature. I think I love you, but I find that my love is alloyed, mottled, and incomplete. I choose to serve you, but find that I bring such ugliness from within that I end up serving myself or some lesser end than you. Lord, I feel defeated at every attempt.

I know I will not always succeed in putting you in your rightful, ruling place in my life, but I desire more than life to try with my redeemed will to choose you above anything in me; to follow you before I do my bidding; to please you before I listen to any human being.

Declare your war, wage your fiercest conflict within me, and by the cross of Christ I will be won for God. Amen.

Resolutions

1. To know that how I think about God determines how I live for God.
2. To agree that man must never be worshiped as God.
3. To be fully convinced that new birth and faith are God's gifts to his children and do not come from anything within man.
4. To confess that nothing in me can move God to save me. He saves me for his own glory alone. Therefore, my salvation and new life are gifts of God to one who was spiritually dead and undeserving.
5. To know that my sinful self hates holiness in others; I judge and condemn others who are more holy than I, because their purity convicts me of my failures and imperfections.
6. To be changed by the truth that I cannot sanctify my sinful self, nor should I ever seek to serve God or practice any Christian virtue by means of my sinful nature. Such actions are destructive to my faith and fruitless for God's kingdom.
7. To agree with God that my heart is filled with wickedness and sin.
8. To be assured that Christ desires to give me rivers of living water that will flow out of my life.

Chapter Six

Self-examination

Thou wilt destroy our emptiness with an amazing fullness.[1]

Not that I have already obtained this or am already perfect, but I press on to make it my own, because Christ Jesus has made me his own. (Philippians 3:12)

What causes quarrels and what causes fights among you? Is it not this, that your passions are at war within you? (James 4:1)

The greatest limitation on holiness being formed in your life is you. To live in obedience to God, to reflect the beauty and character of Jesus Christ in your actions and words, to carry out God's purposes for your life all your life through are all choices you make. Apart from those choices, you will not be holy. Holiness is limited by your character, your sin, and your addictions to praise or porno. People who move toward holiness have such honesty about themselves that when they express it, it takes you aback. They admit they are having inner dialogues about all the same sins as you struggle with. They are never surprised by your admission of a deep, hidden sin or the confession of your besetting, thorn-in-the-flesh sins. They know. They have examined themselves, and they

---

1 Augustine, *Confessions and Enchiridion*, 31, 43; and Augustine of Hippo, *Confessions*, trans. Sheed, 10, 31, p. 195.

know about sin. They aren't fooled by lies or excuses. They know this war because they daily wage war against sin. Christ knew *more* about sin than you ever will because he never sinned. He fought against them all and he was never defeated by even one of them (cf. Hebrews 4:15).

An unending war against sin is exhausting. Sin comes into your life as wild beasts that could tear you limb from limb; with fierce violence they block your way to glory; they stand before you growling, cursing, and threatening you with the loss of everything precious.

The *Divine Comedy* begins with Dante awaking in that dark forest surrounded by vicious wild animals (representing the lusts) blocking the way, opposing any escape. Before he awakes, he knows nothing about these beasts, nothing about his lostness, and nothing about his need for grace. His awareness of the beasts comes to him because he awakens from his numbing sleep one morning in the midst of his life. Williams writes:

> He had himself been full of an interior slumber when he was misled by the deceits of the forest, and there—in such a dangerous gloom—he 're-found himself'—*mi retrovai* ... Some translations give only 'I found myself in a ... wood.' But the original is more intense—'I came to myself again.'[2]

Dante's journey, like yours, begins with self-discovery: he came to himself. There is a point in your life when you awake to certain realities. You know you will die someday. You know that God is to be reckoned with. You know that there is truth and there are lies. You look at your life and the interior voice that makes excuses for how poorly you have done is, if only for a few moments, silenced.

---

2   Williams, *The Figure of Beatrice*, 108. Cp. Edwards, *The Works of Jonathan Edwards*, Vol. 1. xx, Resolution 3, "... to repent of all I can remember, when I come to myself again."

Chapter Six: Self-examination

You see yourself as you are. This vision of yourself is a gift of God that launches you on your journey to God.

You take responsibility for your sin when you know that it is God who examines you and to whom you must give an account. Under his gaze you find the twisted knots of your heart, your lying promises, and your need to control others. Your motives are brought into the light. Now you "come to yourself." Sayers writes:

> There is a point at which dark desire, struggling out of the depths of subconscious, possess the warder who, in Dante's phrase, "Guards the threshold of assent." As a rule, the assent to evil is not recognized until after it has been ratified by the conscious mind.[3]

By this way you gain treasures, priceless treasures, more precious than gold, which perishes. Along the way, you meet horrid people who hurt and abuse you. Your longings befoul every step. You fall and cannot rise alone. You fall again and again, and still yet again you fall! And yet, Grace pulls you forth from the mire. And you are brought to God. Dante writes:

> Had I not passed by such a way, I should not have had this treasure; I should not have had means of joy in the City [of God] to which I approach.[4]

The journey to God must be a journey to holiness. Isaiah heard the angels crying that God is "holy, holy, holy" (Isaiah 6:3; cp. Revelation 4:8). The trifold approbation of God in Hebrew tells us that God is most holy, the holiest of all. To come to the holy God, one must be holy. Becoming holy begins with an examination of the self. Holiness is necessary for those who praise God and dwell in his presence.

---

3 Sayers, *Introductory Papers on Dante,* Vol. 1, 133.
4 Williams, *The Figure of Beatrice,* 229, from Dante's *Convivio.*

Examine yourself

Scripture charts your transformation from being a sin-filled individual to becoming a person who is holy and who lives forever in the presence of Almighty God. Self-examination is a search for evidence of holiness. Self-examination seeks God's opinion of you. It exposes self-deception, tells the truth about your sins, and it seeks the Spirit of God to give comfort and to form holiness within you. The New Testament gives two scenarios in which self-examination should be regularly practiced by the Christian.

First, self-examination precedes a proper observance of the Lord's Table. All who come to the Lord's Table must examine themselves.

> Let a person examine himself, then, and so eat of the bread and drink of the cup. (1 Corinthians 11:28)

And, *second*, self-examination is necessary if one is to be assured of a true and saving faith as a Christian:

> Examine yourselves, to see whether you are in the faith. Test yourselves. Or do you not realize this about yourselves, that Jesus Christ is in you?—unless indeed you fail to meet the test! (2 Corinthians 13:5)

Examination of the self is peppered all through Leviticus 13 and 14. There priests examine conditions that make a worshiper unclean, unholy, and therefore, unqualified to worship a holy God. Leviticus prescribes rites of cleansing and exclusion to those who are "unholy." Paul may have been borrowing those Old Testament pictures of ritual examination as preparation for worship to describe how we are to prepare ourselves to come before God at the Table, and in worship.

A two-sided mirror

The Christian must balance two truths about himself. He is vile and capable of great mischief. And he is great, created in God's image, and capable of fellowship with God. There is both self-abasement and exaltation in the Christian view of man. Pascal writes:

> Christianity is strange: It bids man to recognize that he is vile, and even abominable, and bids him want to be like God. Without such a counterweight his exaltation would make him horribly vain or his abasement horribly abject.[5]

What you know about yourself is your *conscience* (Latin, "*know with*"). What you can "know with" yourself is not what others know about you. Conscience is what no other person knows about you.[6]

Your vile character is seen in your ability to commit sin and then to deny that it was wrong. The conscience informs you that you have committed a crime, but it is incapable of telling you that the crime was wrong. Conscience is a kind of knowing, but it does not have power to reform. The self-deceived admit the fact of sin and yet they deny the harm.

Your self-examination will bring the hidden into the light. You cannot accurately judge yourself. You must bring yourself before God, who judges you. You must have a holy and impartial Judge of your life. You ask God to examine your life every time you receive the bread and cup at the Lord's Table.

The Lord's Table

Self-examination for admission to the Lord's Table requires you to

---

5 Pascal, *Penseés*, XXVI, "Christian Morality," Sect. 351, p. 133.
6 Lewis, *Studies in Words*, 197. Cp., Conscience "bears witness to the fact, say, that we committed murder. It does not tell us that murder is wrong." 190.

perform an honest moral inventory before receiving the bread and the cup. This moral inventory should be explicit and thoroughgoing. Your moral scrutiny should be comprehensive. You have no rational reason to deny or lie about who you are or what you have done. The Lord is not confused or mistaken about your moral condition as a worshiper. He understands your motives completely.

Christ welcomes to his Table only those who examine themselves. It is the *Lord's* Table. Jesus Christ has shed his life-blood for your redemption. The Spirit of God is a fire and a judge of all who come to God in worship. God brings you to a point in your relationship with him where you will hear him ask you the explicit question, "Why did you do it?" Dante comes to that exact point in his journey to God:

> "What do you think of yourself?"....
>
> "Why, why did you do it?"....
>
> He can only falter back his answer:
> "Things transitory with their false delight," weeping
> said I, "enticed my steps aside, soon as your face
> was hidden from my sight."[7]

Self-examination places what you know about yourself, but others don't know about you, before God. Those who are humble earnestly seek God and have nothing to hide.

Augustine said that the sinful self turns worship into "presumption not confession."[8] The sinful self deforms your life with God. It substitutes drudgery, boredom and superciliousness for much that is real and intimate in your walk with God. You presume too much goodness, too little truth in confession. You bear

---

7 Dante, *Purgatory*, trans. Sayers, Canto 21, 34–36, p. 235. Cp. Sayers, *Introductory Papers on Dante*, Vol. 1, 95.

8 Augustine, *Confessions*, Sect. 7, 20, p. 124.

resentments even as you approach God and carry them into the holy place. By the Dark Guest you grasp mercy and grace for yourself, but you are bitter and unforgiving to those who have offended you.

It should be that when you come to the Lord's Table, the Spirit would illuminate some darkness within, perhaps some memory may be brought to mind of a particular sin or you could be convicted once more about a besetting, persistent sin you have struggled with for a long time—or you could be stirred to consider again a deep wound of your soul that was suffered at the hand of another person or by a blow from providence. The Spirit could force into God's light some self-focused longing that is not God's will, but you panted after it anyway. As you come to the Table, the Lord is there, displaying it all in the open. There you choose, by the Spirit, to put the sin to death, to die to self, and to live for Christ. That would be killing your sinful self. That is war.

Meeting the lord at his Table, you are devastated and caressed at the same moment. It is not so much that you examine yourself as it is that you are examined by God. The Table is a gift of grace to break pride, to correct sin, to quiet your tongue, to cleanse your thoughts, to corral your wild lusts, your greed, and your pride. You never feel less deserving or more loved than at the table.

A holy man will not hide his sin but will confess it. He will not presume he is good but will confess that God alone is good. He will not imitate a godly person; he will be a godly person. If you look at yourself apart from God, you will either congratulate or damn yourself. God has another outcome in mind. Richard Foster writes:

> If the examination is solely self-examination, we will always end up with excessive praise or blame. But under the search-light of the great Physician we can expect only good always.[9]

---

9   Foster, *Prayer*, 30.

Must I come again and examine myself at the Table of Christ? Must I go through that again? Have I not looked deeply into my heart enough? Can't I be done with this? Yes, you must come again. And, yes, you must go through it again. No, you haven't looked enough into your heart. And no, you cannot be done with self-examination until you go to Heaven.

Augustine prays:

> [That] I might be able to discern the difference there is between presumption and confession, between those who see what the goal is but do not see the way, and [those who see] the Way which leads to that country of blessedness, which we are meant not only to know but to dwell in.[10]

Self-examination at the Table is "abandoning one's earlier life and behavior."[11] What God says about your words, you say. What God judges in your heart, you judge. But what is more, you begin to mirror to God the riches of his mercy to you. You receive, embrace, and adore his wisdom and truth about your life. There is a smiling agreement with the most terrible assessment of your heart. You experience the relinquishment of your will, words, actions, and thoughts under his scrutiny.

The Table of the Lord is the most terrible, glorious place on Earth. It is not a judgment seat or altar, but a place of breaking bread with your heavenly Lord. It is not sacrifice offered again, not a Mass, but the grace-overwhelmed believer's safest place on Earth, in bread and cup.

The worshiper who examines himself calls what is evil evil, and he calls what is good good. He is not wise in his own eyes. A prophet sang of this:

---

10 Augustine, *Confessions*, 7, 20, p. 124.
11 Augustine, *On Christian Teaching*, Sect. 1, 36.

> Woe to those who call evil good and good evil, who put darkness for light and light for darkness, who put bitter for sweet and sweet for bitter! Woe to those who are wise in their own eyes, and shrewd in their own sight! (Isaiah 5:20–21)

Of course you should think about what you've done! *Of course* you should look inside. *Of course* you should admit your guilt and sin. Nothing could be more necessary! Because Christ paid the penalty for your sins, you must understand them, admit them, confess them, hate them, and die to them.

Sin's secrets

The value of *The Divine Comedy* for self-examination is in how Dante so clearly illustrates the manifold variety of human sin. For instance, one story had him viciously casting aspersions at a group of sinners in Hell. He then turned to curse yet another group he found to be even more despicable. He stood there repeatedly condemning, vilifying, and castigating the pathetic Hell-dwellers.

Only moments later we watch our hero fall into a worse pit, a more horrifying and putrefying pit than the one in which he had so heartlessly judged those who had fallen before him. Sayers explains Dante's tragic hypocrisy:

> Between our admiration and our indignation, between our recognition that Barratry [filing persistent baseless lawsuits for profit, or a ship's captain mismanaging his vessel to cause his owner loss] is worse than Simony [charging exorbitant interest on loans] and our strong disposition to countenance and practice it so far as is reasonable, there might appear some contradiction. Is it possible that we are hypocritical in these matters?

> ... in escaping from the devils of the Fifth Ditch [the place of the greedy], he and Virgil fall promptly into the [Sixth] Ditch of the Hypocrites who walk in leaden cloaks, gilded and glittering.[12]

This is the dilemma of the one who confesses his sins apart from grace. A true worshiper would have a different result. For example, he would come to worship God and leave ashamed of his pride, not puffed up with it. Or he would come to pray but would leave crushed when he grasped how selfish, careless, insipid, crass, and foolish his prayers truly were.

Perhaps you come to doubt God's goodness to you when life is hard, painful, or uncertain. As a spiritual worshiper, you would leave God's presence astonished that he could love you despite the many ways you despised his intentions and hated his will. God's faithfulness never stopped *you* from despising what he called you to live through, though he was with you, and in you, through every sigh and tear. Then you see yourself and know you walk in a leaden cloak and a gilded, glittering robe, and you fall to your knees in true worship of the God of grace. Why he did not breathe you back into the dust (Genesis 2:7) for how greatly you grieve him by your sin, is a great and lofty mystery.

Now you worship. And you worship the God who loves you irrespective of your sin, vapid prayers, presumptuousness, arrogance, foolishness, and your massive ego. The examination of self causes a reality-based view of you standing awestruck in the personal, intimate, knowing, presence of God. You gain a right view of yourself and of God. Examination is about perception, thinking, reasoning, or reckoning.[13]

> Holy Father, you know every molecule of my body, every thought of my mind, every love of my heart.

---

12 Dante, *Hell*, trans. Sayers, 145–146.
13 Owen, *The Holy Spirit*, 155–162.

I pray you would help me to exchange my view of myself with your view of me.

Why, Great Savior, do I neglect the hope of the Gospel: your love, your promises, your faithfulness, my adoption as a child of God, the assurance that nothing can separate me from your love? Why do I who am rich in grace, still live in darkness, chains, poverty, and weakness? In my sin, I am the greatest fool. In my sin, I am blind, deaf, and lost.

Teach me to be so focused on you, Great Father, that I may die to myself and to my sin. May I be freed from sin's chains and seek in you what is holy, good, and perfect. Your holiness illumines my every flaw. It burns them all in a purifying fire.

I desire, Holy Lord, not only be free of my ensnaring sins, but to die to them; not merely to receive your mercy and forgiveness, but to be filled with your grace and then to live in the freedom, joy, and fullness of your Holy Spirit. By my Savior Jesus Christ, I ask. Amen.

The assurance of salvation

Self-examination in 2 Corinthians 13:5 calls you to seek evidence that you are a Christian. By this examination of yourself, you are either confirmed that Christ lives in you, or you fail the test and prove that you are not a believer. What is at stake is eternal life and death.

It matters very little what you think of yourself regarding your salvation. Judas kissed Christ, and he was damned. What matters is that the assurance of salvation can be inwardly known. This assurance is a gift of the Spirit to those who are true Christians.

> The Spirit himself bears witness with our spirit that we are children of God. (Romans 8:16)

> ... to an inheritance that is imperishable, undefiled, and unfading, kept in heaven for you, who by God's power are being guarded through faith for a salvation ready to be revealed in the last time. (1 Peter 1:4–5)

> I write these things to you who believe in the name of the Son of God that you may know that you have eternal life. (1 John 5:13)

Paul warned that false believers may "fail the test." True believers would have confidence in their salvation. Assurance cannot be given to you by another person. It is forged in your faith and heart and it is confirmed by the Holy Spirit and the Word of God.

> And because you are sons, God has sent the Spirit of his Son into our hearts, crying, "Abba! Father!" (Galatians 4:6; cf. Romans 8:15)

Augustine records his self-examination before he became a Christian. His life was a mess. At first he failed this test:

> For I had begun to wish to appear wise, and indeed this was the fullness of my punishment; and I did not weep for my state but was badly puffed up with my knowledge.[14]

---

14 Augustine, *Confessions*, 123.

Chapter Six: Self-examination 107

Dante met Francesca in Hell. She was beautiful, gracious, full of many noble qualities, and damned. Hell is a place you know, with people who are familiar. You recognize her. Sayers writes about Francesca:

> ... all the good in there; the charm, the courtesy, the instant response to affection, the grateful eagerness to please; but also all the evil; the easy yielding, the inability to say No, the intense self-pity.[15]

Did she know she was lost? Did she not look inward? Did she know that her self-pity could not atone? Those who are lost should see their danger and seek the Savior, who alone teaches them to say "No" to sin and be done with their self-pity.

Augustine writes that love is a good evidence of saving grace:

> The person who lives a just and holy life is one who is a sound judge of these things. He is also a person who has ordered his love, so that he does not love what it is wrong to love, or fail to love what should be loved, or love too much what should be loved less (or love too little what should be loved more), or love two things equally if one of them should be loved either less or more than the other, or love things, either more or less if they should be loved equally.[16]

What is it that you truly love? Do you love people and causes appropriately? Are you, in your imbalanced loves, like Francesca, frighteningly incapable of saying "No"? Can you wisely distinguish between a higher good and a lower good in your affections? Do you know the difference between the good and the best in the use

---

15 Sayers, in Dante, *Hell*, her note on Canto 1, 94, p. 102.
16 Augustine, *On Christian Teaching*, Sect. 1, 59.

of your time on Earth? Are you clear about what is good versus what is evil? These matters will be sorted out rather quickly in a believer who is putting the sinful self to death. If your sinful nature is healthy, you will always be confused about whom and what you love and how much you love them.

The sinful self keeps your loves confused. It substitutes a lower love for a higher one. It drives desire to a level of mastery in your life, where you choose the passion and ignore the coming judgment. By your Dark Guest's influence, you can put anything of value in your life at risk, to have, but for an instant, the very thing that God hates.

Passing the test

The Christian life consists of an ordering of your affections—who and what you love, and how much you love everything and everyone. What you used to love you love no longer in the same way. What you did not love before you now love with a love so different, so deep and abiding, nothing in the world compares with it. You are able to say goodbye to the world. You are letting go of what you used to be passionately attached to.

You now love people differently. The people who share your affection for Christ become dearer to you than any earthly family. Some in your world who have been immeasurably cruel and hurtful to you, you find room now in your heart to pray for and even love. Your loves are now ordered by the Spirit who dwells within. You imitate God:

> Therefore be imitators of God, as beloved children. And walk in love, as Christ loved us and gave himself up for us, a fragrant offering and sacrifice to God. (Ephesians 5:1–2)

> If you love me, you will keep my commandments. (John 14:15)

Self-examination and self-denial

The Christian examines the self to seek evidence of self-denial. Self-denial is defined as the set of decisions in which you say "No" to your sinful self and desires. If you look inside and do not see your own cross, nor experience your own crucifixion, if there is no dying to self, no killing of your sin nature, then you have failed this test.

You have died with Christ; you can live only in him. The proof of faith comes by the eradication of self. Dietrich Bonhoeffer writes:

> Jesus has graciously prepared the way for this word by speaking of self-denial. Only when we have become completely oblivious of self are we ready to bear the cross for his sake.
>
> ... If Jesus had not so graciously prepared us for this word, we should have found it to be unbearable. But by preparing us for it he has enabled us to receive even as hard as this as a word of grace. It comes to us in the joy of discipleship and confirms us in it.[17]

Self-examination ought to find the God-work of self-denial in you. When you look inside, you find that Jesus' words explain just about everything about you:

> And he said to all, "If anyone would come after me, let him deny himself and take up his cross daily and follow me." (Luke 9:23; cf. Matthew 16:24–26, J.B. Phillips)[18]

---

17 Bonhoeffer, *The Cost of Discipleship*, 88.
18 Phillips, *New Testament in Modern English*.

Resolutions

1. To see my holiness informing me about my sin and God's remedy for it, rather than becoming a means of criticizing or judging others or of declaring myself a failure as a Christian.
2. To form holiness in my life through the Word of God and the Spirit of God dwelling in me, apart from my ability or power.
3. To know how complete is my infection with sin.
4. To renounce and to repudiate my conscience as a means of reforming or sanctifying my character. Holiness is from the Lord alone. My conscience is an unreliable guide to holiness.
5. To hear God ask me about my sin, "Why did you do it?"
6. To desire more than life itself, the willingness and honest longing to be examined by God.
7. To know that assurance of salvation is a gift of God to every child of God.
8. To experience the testing of my true and saving faith in the ordering of my loves for God and for others.
9. To search for the evidence of self-denial as a word of grace to me and a profitable proof of saving faith.

Chapter Seven

Repentance

No, I tell you; but unless you repent, you will all likewise perish. (Luke 13:3)

The soul is reformed after repentance, by which the soul kills off its earlier evil character .... [1]

Yet, though we say so formally, there is in us, since the Fall, a kind of necessity of sin, and repentance is by no means so necessary. [2]

If you are to sin less, you must repent more. The sinful self hates and actively opposes the grace of repentance. Mortification—killing sin—begins with the grace-empowered act of repentance. You will never die to any sin unless you first repent of it.

You will never increase in your holiness without repentance. You will never go to Heaven if you have not personally experienced the reforming, renewing, and sin-purging power of repentance. Repentance is a mark of a true and saving faith.

Repentance identifies, understands, condemns, and turns from sin. The greatest enemy of indwelling sin is Spirit-empowered repentance. Sin's defensive tactics against its greatest foe are:

---

1   Augustine, *On Christian Teaching*, Sect. 1, 36.
2   Williams, *The Figure of Beatrice*, 147.

> To delay repentance
>
> To deny the need for repentance
>
> To minimize your need to be rid of actual sin
>
> To redefine the nature of sin
>
> To limit your understanding of sin
>
> To blame the consequences of your sin on others
>
> To refuse to accept responsibility for your sin, and
>
> To keep you blind regarding the enslaving nature of your sin.

If you are to gain victory over indwelling sin, repentance must be a daily, persistent, non-negotiable, pervasive, comprehensive, completely honest, rigorous, thorough, Spirit-led, Word-directed, foundational, essential, never-ending, joyful, grace-based, on-your-knees, and from-the-heart warfare waged against your sinful nature. If you want to be defeated by sin, don't repent.

You are not forced to repent. It is something that you are free *not* to do. Some people don't repent. The Apostle Paul faced this fact with the Corinthians:

> I fear that when I come again my God may humble me before you, and I may have to mourn over many of those who sinned earlier and have not repented of the impurity, sexual immorality, and sensuality that they have practiced. (2 Corinthians 12:21)

Some people in the Corinthian church ought to have repented of their sins, but they hadn't. They had "repented" (as a one-time event) when they became Christians. But the daily, continuous, and persistent repentance, that is emblematic of the Christian's life was not present.

In a local church, when the focus is solely on conversion, initial repentance is all that is taught. But repentance is much more than acknowledging before God and his church, 15 seconds before you are baptized, that you are a sinner. Repentance is also how you live as a Christian for the rest of your life. Repentance begins when you are saved, and it ends when you die.

Repentance, crucial but not mandatory

The Fall creates in you a kind of necessity to sin. Williams said, "Repentance is by no means so necessary."[3] You decline opportunities to repent. You cloud your minds with excuses and permissions that delay repentance.

Repentance, it is sad to say, is not so necessary. But it is necessary *if* you are to live for God. God doesn't compel you to turn from your sins. Repentance is a decision you make.

Christians who believe that repentance is a once-in-a-lifetime experience will live ugly lives. That error makes spiritual growth very difficult; it denies your identity in Christ; it grieves the Holy Spirit of God; it renders you fruitless in service to God; it negates your testimony; it mars the Gospel; it denies your identity as a son or daughter of God; it obscures your heavenly home; it makes you a friend of the world; it creates cooperation with the demonic forces to thwart and denude the power of the Gospel to change your life to be conformed to the divine nature (2 Peter 1); and it crucifies afresh your Lord Jesus Christ (Hebrews 6:6). Repentance may not be necessary, but it is absolutely essential if you are to honor God and live a holy life.

---

3   Williams, *The Figure of Beatrice*, 147.

Repentance and self-examination

Repentance is turning from sin, confessing it, and turning to God for mercy and forgiveness.

> Remember therefore from where you have fallen; repent, and do the works you did at first. If not, I will come to you and remove your lampstand from its place, unless you repent. (Revelation 2:5; cf. Luke 17:4)

Scriptures often ties repentance to conversion. The words are almost synonymous. Repentance accompanies faith and new birth. Repentance is how you began your Christian experience. No one becomes a Christian apart from repentance. The conversation with God about your sin is the crucial starting point of the Christian life. Christ died for your sins. Repentance acknowledges your sins against God, the fact that you cannot save yourself, and that Christ is your only hope for forgiveness and life.

> No, I tell you; but unless you repent, you will all likewise perish." (Luke 13:3, cp. 13:5)

> ... and that repentance and forgiveness of sins should be proclaimed in his name to all nations, beginning from Jerusalem. (Luke 24:47)

> Repent therefore, and turn again, that your sins may be blotted out. (Acts 3:19)

> When they heard these things they fell silent. And they glorified God, saying, "Then to the Gentiles also God has granted repentance that leads to life." (Acts 11:18)[4]

---

[4] Cp. Luke 5:32; Acts 26:20; 2 Timothy 2:25; Hebrews 6:1; and 2 Peter 3:9.

Repentance is essential to and concurrent with conversion. Those who believe turn from their sins, are sorrowful over them, and turn to God in newness of life. At the point at which a person is saved, he repents of his sins.

But repentance is also used to summarize the entire Christian life. A Christian continually repents of his sins.

> As it is, I rejoice, not because you were grieved, but because you were grieved into repenting. For you felt a godly grief, so that you suffered no loss through us. (2 Corinthians 7:9)

> Those whom I love, I reprove and discipline, so be zealous and repent. (Revelation 3:19)

Repentance is not merely inaugural, it is continual.[5] Considering either the initial repentance unto life, or any subsequent repentance afterward, repentance begins with an "unclouded vision of sin." Sayers writes:

> Dante, when he made the unclouded vision of sin the first effects of the return to innocence, may have meant that this experience must necessarily befall any spirit that is fully purged.[6]

Dante's *Purgatory* finds its name from Roman Catholic medieval theology, but what is described in his poem is the repentance and purgation of sin that every biblical Christian could understand. His poem was a testimony from a believer who was led by grace to be freed from the power, dominion, enslaving captivity,

---

[5] Some characters in the Bible who repented still experienced the consequences of their sins. E.g. Achan in Joshua 7:11 and 20; cf. David in 2 Samuel 11 and 12; Psalm 32 and 51; cf. 2 Corinthians 11:21.

[6] Sayers, *Introductory Papers on Dante*, Vol. 1, 97.

and destruction of sin.

> Purgation is what happens to the soul which, accepting judgment, moves out of illusion into reality, and this is the subject of the *Purgatorio*.[7]

Moving sin out of illusion and into reality is extraordinarily difficult soul-work. The sinful self calls the evil good and good evil. Sin can be outward rebellion against God's law (as in lying or adultery), or it can be inward sin seen in pride and Phariseeism. Everything you do is infected by sin. Your best acts of obedience are smeared with its taint. A man who believes his service to God is acceptable is in far greater danger than the man who cries, "Lord, be merciful to me, *the* sinner."[8] The sinful man's cry takes the fact of sin and he owns that truth about himself as his moniker—"the sinner."

Ananias and Sapphira believed they could lie to the Holy Spirit if it were for a good cause. They thought they were doing a good thing in selling a piece of property and giving a portion of it to the local church. They lied to the church and to the Holy Spirit about the sale price and kept back some of the proceeds for themselves. They gave the money to the church so they would be seen as generous people. They died for that sin (cf. Acts 5:1–11). Most certainly it was a surprise to Ananias and Sapphira to learn that the Apostles and God disapproved of their gift to the church, just before they dropped dead. They thought they were doing a good deed. They believed the lie that you can lie to God and get away with it.

Apart from Christ, every righteous act on your part is cause for his anger. Remember the words of St. Augustine:

> The self is filled with presumption not confession.[9]

---

7   Ibid., 72.
8   Cp. Luke 18:13, the definite article is in the Greek.
9   Augustine, *Confessions*, 7, 20, p. 124.

Chapter Seven: Repentance 117

Repentance comes from your *redeemed heart*. You aren't merely sorry you were caught. You grieve your sin and are broken by it. You know that it is out of your sinful heart that all of your sin flows (cf. Mark 7:21–23). You now grieve, from the deepest place within your soul, that you are a sinner who has offended God:

> We have all become like one who is unclean, and all our righteous deeds are like a polluted garment. (Isaiah 64:6)

> And to the one who does not work but believes in him who justifies the ungodly, his faith is counted as righteousness. (Romans 4:5)

Victory over indwelling sin begins with confession. After confession comes repentance. Only then is mortification—putting the sin to death—possible. A sinner is therefore "purged," not only of the sinful deeds, but of the root and cause of that sin.

> For godly grief produces a repentance that leads to salvation without regret, whereas worldly grief produces death. (2 Corinthians 7:10)

> And we all, with unveiled face, beholding the glory of the Lord, are being transformed into the same image from one degree of glory to another. For this comes from the Lord who is the Spirit. (2 Corinthians 3:18)

Repentance is formed by your understanding of God. You need God's Word flowing into your life every day. True repentance begins when God speaks truth to you about your life, "Your word is truth" (John 17:17b).

Loving Redeemer, Glorious God, you bore with my sins long before I knew them. You heard my prayers and received them for Christ's sake, even when they carried more presumption and selfish longings in them than worship or praise. Demons cried out for mercy, as I have done, but they never believed your goodness, nor contemplated your love.

Deliver me, my grace-possessed Father, from my sin-protecting prayers, my self-serving cries to your throne, and my perverse demands that you bless me, when long ago you promised blessing to all who love you and you sealed your promise with the blood of your Son.

I petition your throne for gifts that would kill me, and you must decline most of what I seek. Grant me only what will bring honor to your name and good to my soul, by your grace and for your glory.

Teach me, by whatever means you deem best, to abandon myself and my safety, that I may trust your will in all things, believe your goodness, and love whatever means you choose to bring glory to your name through me.

Hide me, Holy King, under the shadow of your glory. Keep me close to you—no matter what may be the cost to me. I ask this because Christ loved your will more than his life, as should I. Amen.

Teaching our tongues to confess

Christians from long ago had a much different view of themselves living in the presence of Almighty God than we have today. Today the self is to be esteemed, nurtured, and affirmed. We are taught to be "true to ourselves." We are encouraged to "find ourselves."

Christians of long ago saw the Dark Guest not as something to be esteemed, nurtured, and discovered but as something to be wrestled with and killed. Here are some prayers from *The Valley of Vision*, a selection of Christian prayers from about 300 years ago:

> It is a good day to me when thou givest me a glimpse of myself; sin is my greatest evil, but thou are my greatest good; I have cause to loath myself, and not seek self-honour, for no one desires to commend his own dunghill....

> O my crucified but never wholly mortified sinfulness! O my life-long damage and daily shame! O my indwelling and besetting sins! Destroy, O God, the Dark Guest within whose hidden presence makes my life a hell. Yet thou hast not left me here without grace. The cross still stands and meets my needs in the deepest straits of the soul ... there is no treasure so wonderful as the continuous experience of thy grace toward me which alone can subdue the risings of sin within: Give me more of it.[10]

Today's doctrine of the Christian life is supposed to make us feel good, loved, accepted, and forgiven. Contrast that view with the faith experience contained in these old prayers. Those 17th- and 18th-century Christians saw God as the bedrock of their faith. They waged warfare daily against the Dark Guest. So strong was their

---

10   Bennett, ed., *The Valley of Vision*, "The Dark Guest," 122, 127.

conflict with their sin that the language of their prayers shocks us today. It is violent, harsh, and aggressive! [11]

The Puritan prayers go so far as to suggest that only by facing the horrid truth about you are you finally able to gain God's power and his victory over the sin that makes your "life a hell." The Puritans knew that though you are forgiven, living the Christian life is a trial. Repentance is beginning with Christ, continuing with Christ, living for Christ, and finishing with Christ. But this daily, relentless, painfully difficult struggle is rarely spoken of today.

The *Paradise* gave a portrait of the future consummation of Christ with his people at the Wedding Feast of the Lamb that is adumbrated by the Lord's Supper:

> O fellowship of the elect who sup
> With Christ the Lamb, who doth so nourish you
> That full to overflowing is your cup,
>
> If God by grace admits this man unto
> The broken meats that from your table fall,
> Before the hour prescribed by death is due,
>
> The boundless measure of his love recall,
> Bedew him with some drops! your fountainhead,
> Whence comes what he thinks, is perpetual.[12]

Modern faith struggles to speak about the internal conflict between the old sinful self and the renewed self. Despite our stammering, that conflict must be active if we are to become more like Jesus Christ. We need help to live with the reality that we love both

---

11   Cp. Edwards, *The Works of Jonathan Edwards*, Volume 1, xxi. Resolution 22, "... to endeavor to obtain for myself as much happiness, in the world, as I possibly can, with all the power, might, vigor, and vehemence, yea violence, I am capable of ...."

12   Dante, *Paradise*, trans. Sayers and Reynolds, Canto 24, 1–9, p. 265.

Christ and our sin. Yet that pitiable state is the condition of everyone who believes. It would do us well to cry out to God with wails for help for our sins! Listen to the heart-song found in another old prayer:

> O Lord, Bend my hands and cut them off,
>   for I have often struck thee with a wayward will,
> when these fingers should embrace thee by faith.
>
> I am not yet weaned from all created glory,
>   honour, wisdom, and esteem of others,
> for I have a secret motive to eye my name in all I do.[13]

Your Christian faithfulness, effectiveness, fruitfulness, and obedience depend upon your successful war against the Dark Guest. Another prayer from *The Valley of Vision* tells the griefs of sanctification:

> O Changeless God, Under the conviction of thy Spirit
>   I learn that the more I do, the worse I am,
>   the more I know, the less I know,
>   the more holiness I have, the more sinful I am,
>   the more I love, the more there is to love.
> O Wretched man that I am![14]

These old prayers strike the heart. Once you arrive at the place of this kind of soul-honest truth in your repentance, the road is illuminated toward greater intimacy with God. You can now understand yourself and you can see God more clearly. The light will always illuminate your darkness. Truth will always confront lies and your stupid games.

With light and truth come hope and victory. With darkness and lies come slavery and a hell within. A hell within believers in Christ.

---

13 Bennett, ed., *The Valley of Vision*, 126.

14 Ibid., 128.

This ought not to be!

> Who among you fears the Lord
>   and obeys the voice of his servant?
> Let him who walks in darkness
>   and has no light
> trust in the name of the Lord
>   and rely on his God. (Isaiah 50:10)

The hope of your salvation is that God is working and shall work in you every day of your life.

> Therefore, my beloved, as you have always obeyed, so now, not only as in my presence but much more in my absence, work out your own salvation with fear and trembling, for it is God who works in you, both to will and to work for his good pleasure. (Philippians 2:12–13)

> We want each of you to show this same diligence to the very end, in order to make your hope sure. We do not want you to become lazy, but to imitate those who through faith and patience inherit what has been promised. (Hebrews 6:11–12, NIV)

Half-repentance

Repentance is not merely about the deeds of sin but about their cause. The root of sin is broken only by a complete repentance. Sayers writes:

> Hell is concerned with fruits, but purgatory with the roots of sin.[15]

---

[15] Sayers, in Dante, *Purgatory*, 15.

Repentance is turning from sin and to God. Half-repentance is either turning from sin but not turning to God, or turning to God without turning from your sin. Either kind of half-repentance is the work of the Dark Guest.

Half-repentance that turns from sin but not to God is self-redeeming and self-punishing. The Dark Guest directs you to repent from your sins without God's help. It wants you to identify your sins, to see how damaging they are, but to turn from them in your flesh. Your sinful nature keeps sin and sin's remedy separated.

> Are you so foolish? Having begun by the Spirit, are you now being perfected by the flesh? (Galatians 3:3)

True repentance sees your sin in light of the presence of God. It is God's holiness and his profound, personal hatred of your sin that empowers your repentance—if you love him.

Your sin nature wants you to improve yourself without God's help. You might extinguish a habit and stop a sin for a while. But the end will be bad. You will replace one overt, outward sin with an inward, hidden one.

The other version of half-repentance is when you turn to God for grace and love, but you do not turn from your sin (cf. Romans 6:1ff.) This false repentance separates God from the life of the believer. It accepts grace, but it denies sanctification. It receives love, but it does not turn from sin. This half-repentance drives a wedge between the character of God and the character of the Christian.

True repentance constantly draws the believer's life into alignment with the character of God. You should be something like God in your character:

> For he who sanctifies and those who are sanctified all have one source. That is why he is not ashamed to call them brothers. (Hebrews 2:11)

> Beloved, we are God's children now, and what we will be has not yet appeared; but we know that when he appears we shall be like him, because we shall see him as he is. (1 John 3:2)

Half-repentance claims mercy, but it does not transform the life. It steals grace, but it does not die to self. It accepts the love of God, but not the discipline of God. It accepts regeneration, but not sanctification. It believes in forgiveness of sins, but not the mortification of sins. It wants to have Christ indwelling and the Dark Guest indwelling and at peace with one another.

Christ Jesus did not die so you could be at ease with indwelling sin. Half-repentance is no repentance at all. True repentance begins when, by faith, you lift your eyes to God. There you know him and you understand yourself. Calvin writes:

> Man never achieves a clear knowledge of himself until he has first looked upon God's face, and then descends from contemplating [God] to scrutinize himself.[16]

Future repentance

Every day you rise to remember who you are, what you have done, and to whom you belong. The repentant Christian is honest, humble, and filled with gratitude for mercy.

Repentance moves you from the past to the future. Instead of merely being filled with regret and disappointment about your past sins, you are moved into the future of grace-filled living, forgetting those things which are behind (cf. Philippians 3:13). Every day you should do as much repenting as you have sins to repent of.

Repenting isn't holding your hands behind your back and crossing your fingers while you say to God, "I *promise* I won't sin

---

16 Calvin, *Institutes*, 2, 2, 11, pp. 269–270.

anymore!" It is taking responsibility for your actions, identifying them as sin against the God who saved you and whom you love more than life. It is turning from that sin and hating it. It is turning to God for mercy and restoration.

Neither is repentance dredging up every sin you can remember and wallowing in that huge pile of dung so you will feel bad. Repentance is not a pity party. It is killing the Dark Guest.

Your horrid, sinful self will bring sins into your mind and into your actions. When that happens, repent of the sins, name them, and confess to God what you did. But go further and understand what it would mean for you to turn from those sins for the rest of your life. Calculate what repentance involves.

Repentance is not stopping a sin for a few days. It is turning from sin. Totally. You plan never to do it again.

> ... and to put on the new self, created after the likeness of God in true righteousness and holiness. (Ephesians 4:24)

Sin will certainly spring up again later. We all fail or fall after we have repented. When you fall, repent *again*. You now have new information about how you miscalculated the difficulty of repentance that last time. You have a new appreciation of how truly, massively stupid you are, and how much weaker you are than you had presumed. This time you can repent better. There must come a point of victory over that sin if you are truly repenting. There is no sin in your life that you *must* commit.

> No temptation has overtaken you that is not common to man. God is faithful, and he will not let you be tempted beyond your ability, but with the temptation he will also provide the way of escape, that you may be able to endure it. (1 Corinthians 10:13)

You are able, by Christ's blood and the filling presence of the Holy Spirit, to repent continually.

> Bear fruit in keeping with repentance. (Matthew 3:8)

> I have not come to call the righteous but sinners to repentance. (Luke 5:32)

> ... and said to them, "Thus it is written, that the Christ should suffer and on the third day rise from the dead, and that repentance and forgiveness of sins should be proclaimed in his name to all nations, beginning from Jerusalem." (Luke 24:46–27)

> The Lord is not slow to fulfill his promise as some count slowness, but is patient toward you, not wishing that any should perish, but that all should reach repentance. (2 Peter 3:9)

Resolutions

1. To know that there is a direct correlation between the extent of my repentance and the holiness in my life.
2. To be assured that the Christian life is a life of continual repentance.
3. To believe with all my heart and rejoice in my soul that repentance is the song of the redeemed.
4. To know that repentance leads me not only to my sin, but to the root and cause of my sin. The root and cause of my sin must be sought in repentance.
5. To search my heart how God may make my repentance full and complete. To turn completely from my sin and turn completely to God in my repentance.
6. To know repentance requires that I will seek with every fiber of my being not to commit a sin again, but to die to it.
7. To begin my repentance by looking at the face of God (in the person of the Lord Jesus Christ).
8. To experience the victory of Christ in that there is no sin that I must now commit; neither is there any sin over which I cannot gain victory through Christ my Savior! I am no longer a slave to sin, but I am a slave to God.

Chapter Eight

The Love of God, the Lordship of Christ, and the Will of God

Joy in God is impossible without the Mediator.[1]

The unity of love and will.[2]

The true love of God captures your affections.[3] It takes prisoners and it enslaves you to the God of mercy. It sets you free from sin's corrupting and damning captivity.

Remember how enslaved you were to the sins that captured your heart? Remember how powerless you were when you tried to break sin's chains on your life?

> ... but I see in my members another law waging war against the law of my mind and making me captive to the law of sin that dwells in my members. (Romans 7:23)

The love of God sets you free from your captivity.

---

1   Augustine, *Confessions*, Sect. 7, 18, p. 122.
2   Dante, *Paradise*, "Introduction," by Barbara Reynolds, 21.
3   Edwards, *The Religious Affections*.

> But now that you have been set free from sin and have become slaves of God, the fruit you get leads to sanctification and its end, eternal life. (Romans 6:22)

God's love teaches you what to love and what to hate. Coming into the love of God not only teaches you, it captures you so that your heart begins to love as God loves. You learn to love what God loves, as your heart aligns with the values, the goals, the purposes of God's love for the world. God's love is strong, unapologetic, and forever holy. Marshall writes:

> When fully assured of God's love, you will respond by living a holy life. [4]

God's love is redeeming, saving, and rescuing to the uttermost those who have faith in Christ. The love of God illuminates, captivates, controls, constrains, resists, conquers, kills, crucifies, touches, nurtures, comforts, and saves. The love of God comes into a believer's life, and the Christian meets God. Paul sings of the love of God:

> Who shall separate us from the love of Christ? Shall tribulation, or distress, or persecution, or famine, or nakedness, or danger, or sword? As it is written,
>
> "For your sake we are being killed all the day long; we are regarded as sheep to be slaughtered."
>
> No, in all these things we are more than conquerors through him who loved us. For I am sure that neither death nor life, nor angels nor rulers, nor things present nor things to come, nor powers, nor

---

4   Marshall, *The Gospel Mystery of Sanctification*, 30.

height nor depth, nor anything else in all creation, will be able to separate us from the love of God in Christ Jesus our Lord. (Romans 8:35–39)

God's love is rich beyond measure, stronger than Hell's gates, more beautiful than the angels can sing (Revelation 5:9, cp. 14:3). Nothing in the universe is greater in value or contains more of God's glory than the love of God demonstrated in Christ Jesus. Nothing is stronger, holier, wiser, or more perfect. Nothing in all creation. And his love is in you.

The love of God

The love of God is the controlling force in a Christian's life. God's love for you is the primary motive for your holiness. You desire to be holy because you love God above all else, and you desire to be more and more like him in your character.

It would be abominable for a person to receive God's love in salvation, to be declared just in God's eyes, to have the righteousness of Jesus Christ given to him by faith, and not have it change him. How could someone believe in the love of God for himself and not experience the substantial change that God's love brings to bear upon everything in his world? For one to claim God's love but to experience no substantial change in his life, indicates that that person did not know the love of God in any redeeming sense. God's redeeming love changes everything in your world.

This is not to say that a Christian cannot question the love of God, the stings of God's providence, or the purposes of God in severe sufferings or sorrows. We all have doubts and can be shaken by trials. But we must resolve these questions or those who believe would never suffer; or those who suffer would never believe. Many believers who suffer horrific trials are faithful in their sorrows and they do so with great confidence and with astounding joy.

The enemy of God's love

The self is the enemy of the love of God. If it may not bring you to doubt God's love for you—a love so brilliantly demonstrated in Christ that there ought to be no question—it will bring you to attempt in some God-offending way to qualify for it, to earn it, or to justify his ineffable love for you.

The human self is at enmity with the love of God. The Pharisees represent much that is wrong in you and in me. They were religious to the extreme, the chief opponents of God when he came back to his own Temple. They worked tireless to destroy Jesus who was God in human flesh. They were alien to the grace of God. The Pharisees wanted to follow their complex system of rules and laws and, like modern terrorists, to implement their rules with the sword or with heavy rocks to the head (cf. Acts 7:58).

The Pharisee's god seeks to control, not to liberate. Their god demands changes in your life that you must create within yourself—a false set of standards that never changes a heart or forges a resemblance to God's true character. The Pharisee's god whitewashes death instead of giving life to the dead. Their god's will is oppressive, accusing, and must be enforced with maximum control or with violence.

Who would willingly submit to the will of the god created by the Pharisees' fanaticism? Who would want to live under such a meticulous regime in which religion is condensed to rules instead of a relationship with God? Such a system flaunts the superiority of extreme compliance to laws and control, over a joyous, loving response to our loving God whose redemption won us completely and for all eternity by the cross and the resurrection.

The true love of God shreds the Pharisee's heart by the purest holiness, the righteousness of Christ, the sweetest and deepest of loves, and a repudiation of any suggestion of human goodness before God. Those who know the God of love surrender their wills to God's. There is no safer, wiser, or better choice than to obey the will of God. In *Paradise*, Dante, after a long and agonizing journey, lovingly relinquished his will to God's:

> That light doth so transfer a man's whole bent,
>   That never to another sight or thought
> Would he surrender, with his own consent;
>
> For everything the will has ever sought
>   Is gathered there, and there is every quest
> Made perfect, which apart from it falls short.[5]

The love of God creates within the worst of guilty sinners a heart of confidence, a hope that can't be shaken or destroyed, and courage within one who was once condemned by his own sins, to stand and give everything to God and for him, to the praise of his glorious grace. It heals the wounds of the worst of sinners. It adopts as sons and daughters the illegitimate children who now have access to God, communion with God, and the knowledge of God.

The love of God gives the humble believer the personal presence of the Lord Jesus Christ to live in him by the Spirit. He not only knows the love of God but the God of love dwells within his heart.

Repentance must begin with the love of God. Be certain that the love of God has not been diluted, revised, twisted or subtracted. Keep the Pharisee at a distance; use a whip if you must. Seek the full measure of the love of God and the Dark Guest cannot stand. By the overflowing fullness of God's love, your sinful self can die, and your redeemed self can rise at last, to live forever and to love with his love.

> For if we have been united with him in a death like his, we shall certainly be united with him in a resurrection like his. (Romans 6:5)

---

5 Dante, *Paradise*, trans. Sayers and Reynolds, Canto 33, 100–105, p. 346.

The Lordship of Christ

Christ is holy. By faith you are *in him*. Therefore, you are holy only by his imputed perfections. He has given you robes that are white (meaning they were ceremonially clean) because they are washed in the blood of the Lamb (cp. Revelation 7:14). You are able to love God because you are *in Christ Jesus*. This phrase, and varieties of it like *in the Lord* or *in him*, is used more than 200 times in the New Testament.[6]

> There is therefore now no condemnation for those who are in Christ Jesus. (Romans 8:1)

> For as in Adam all die, so also in Christ shall all be made alive.
> (1 Corinthians 15:22)

You cannot live the Christian life in your strength, by your will, or in your power. God has given you the gifts, the graces, and the virtues of his own character (see 2 Peter 1). But those virtues must be exercised by the individual filled with the Spirit of God, prayed for by Jesus Christ, and filled with the strength that God supplies. You are actively obedient, but you are dependent upon God to enliven every choice and to empower every action, to purify every word.

Mortification of sin is an act of the redeemed will.[7] You make choices about your holiness. In every choice, God is working in you both to will and to do his good pleasure (cf. Philippians 2:13).

---

6   Reumann, *Variety and Unity in New Testament Thought*, 78, reports 165 occurrences (cf. Stewart, *A Man in Christ*, passim); Akin, Nelson, Shemm, *A Theology for the Church*, 688, reports 216 occurrences, including "in him," "in Christ," "in the Lord." The author's count, using the ESV, "in him" 79, "in Christ" 95, "in the Lord" 53, for 227 verses, counting only affirmative uses of the phrases; adding "in the name" 24, and "in Jesus" 10, the total is 261.

7   Owen, *Overcoming Sin and Temptation*, 62.

Yielding your will to Christ as Lord is to acknowledge that he has power and authority to control and direct your life as he wishes.

Practically speaking, you must choose to live a holy life. Theologically speaking, you could never choose holiness or make even one holy decision apart from Christ's cross, the Spirit's fullness, or the Word of God's instruction.

Choosing holiness and loving God

An infallible relationship exists between the presence of the Holy Spirit indwelling the believer and the fruit (the results, the manifestation, the evidence) of the Spirit in that life. This is God's will for us in every case, in every person, in every circumstance of life. Even the thief on the cross exercised love, joy, peace, kindness, goodness, meekness, and self-control (maybe more), and he believed for only a few moments before his death (cf. Luke 23:39ff.).

We also practice active obedience that pours, flies, and flows from the love we have *for* God. Jesus said "If you love me, keep my commandments." (John 14:15). The active obedience that begins with a love *for* God compels the believer to obey God. Not always. Not 100 percent of the time. Not 24/7. But more and more:

> Finally, then, brothers, we ask and urge you in the Lord Jesus, that as you received from us how you ought to walk and to please God, just as you are doing, that you do so more and more. (1 Thessalonians 4:1)

This obedience comes from the love of God for the believer, and the love of the believer for God.

> In this is love, not that we have loved God but that he loved us and sent his Son to be the propitiation for our sins. (1 John 4:10)

> ... but whoever keeps his word, in him truly the love of God is perfected. By this we may know that we are in him .... (1 John 2:5)

God's love for you produces obedience:

> I am the vine; you are the branches. Whoever abides in me and I in him, he it is that bears much fruit, for apart from me you can do nothing. (John 15:5)

You know that nothing can separate you from God (Romans 8:38–39). Nothing can defeat you. You are "more than conquerors," (Philippians 4:13) even when you fall or fail, he is faithful, though you are not. Your love for God is the crucial test of the truth of your claim to be a Christian. Jesus thought it was important. The religious of his day stood condemned by the Son of God because they failed this test:

> But I know that you do not have the love of God within you. (John 5:42)

The love of God is worked out in the measure by which you "do what the Father is doing." Jesus loved the Father by doing what the Father did:

> So Jesus said to them, 'Truly, truly, I say to you, the Son can do nothing of his own accord, but only what he sees the Father doing. For whatever the Father does, that the Son does likewise. (John 5:19)

It is inconceivable that a Christian could love God and not yield his thoughts, will, and emotions to God. This yielding to God's rule is often declared in the Bible:

Chapter Eight: Love, Lordship, and Will

> Do not present your members to sin as instruments for unrighteousness, but present yourselves to God as those who have been brought from death to life, and your members to God as instruments for righteousness. For sin will have no dominion over you, since you are not under law but under grace. (Romans 6:13–14)

> For the love of Christ controls us, because we have concluded this: that one has died for all, therefore all have died; and he died for all, that those who live might no longer live for themselves but for him who for their sake died and was raised. (2 Corinthians 5:14–15)[8]

Everything you own is his. Your life is his to do with as he wishes. Your future is God's, that you might do his will, not yours.

> For if we live, we live to the Lord, and if we die, we die to the Lord. So then, whether we live or whether we die, we are the Lord's. (Romans 14:8)

> If anyone comes to me and does not hate his own father and mother and wife and children and brothers and sisters, yes, and even his own life he cannot be my disciple. (Luke 14:26)

"Hate ... even his own life"! These words make sense only when one sees the conflict between the sinful self and God within the life of every believer. By faith you push away every competitor of the love of God. Christ's Lordship means even family relationships don't have a claim on you as they did before you believed. Family is tremendously important. Believers are commanded to honor

---

8   Cf. 1 Chronicles 16:11; and Psalm 25:4ff.

parents, be committed to their marriages, and love their children. But a Christian loves his family as an expression of his love for God. Walking with God leads one to care for one's family. Family love does not necessarily lead one to God.

The will of God

Doing the will of God from the heart is the Christian's chief goal and highest aspiration. The love of God ought always to result in your obedience to his will (cf. Ephesians 6:6). God's will may cost you your life. It often results in suffering. It can wrench away from you everything you own. It can require from you your health or your family. And it is still good.

Many believers—perhaps the majority—live as Christians, raise their kids, go to church, enjoy their friends, endure their jobs, are reasonably conflict-free, and then they go to Heaven. They experience the love of God as safe, warm, and kind. They know the protection and blessing of the Father for his children. Their adoption into the family of God is hope-filled and productive, fruitful and God-honoring. Perhaps during their entire lives they never experienced anything that conflicted with their knowledge of the Father's love.

Other people are wrested out of comfort, thrown into conflict, engaged in warfare with demons (none you could see), and may not know happiness. Their kids do drugs, their churches fall apart with conflict, and they die suffering painful deaths after living pain-filled lives. The Father's will for them is all they could take. Their faith is almost at the breaking point. They pray, not really from faith, but only because it is all they know to do. The Father's will for them is not what they expected. But they still die believing.

Some Christians live the life of the rich and famous. Others are stabbed by natives. Both ends rest within the will of God. The question is not so much what God's will is for your life, but are you willing to do it, whatever it turns out to be?

... saying, "Father, if you are willing, remove this cup from me. Nevertheless, not my will, but yours, be done." (Luke 22:42)

"Not my will, but yours, be done." The Dark Guest has something to say about that. The Dark Guest wants you to get out of the pain. Jesus asked, "If it be possible, let this cup pass from me —" he did not say, "I refuse to do it." The Dark Guest's will collides with the purposes of God. Jesus gave himself completely to the Father. We struggle every day to reach up to God in our choices. John Piper writes about the failure of self-love:

> The inadequacy of self-love is that its branches do
> not reach up to God.[9]

Something known to the Father, but unknown to you, is at work in the will of God. The Father wants you to do something difficult, but you do not see what purpose it will serve. The Dark Guest will scream that it will be pointless, stupid, a waste to suffer needlessly. The Dark Guest protests that much of God's will is unknown or unexplained to you and, therefore, yielding to it is utterly foolish.

Jesus knew the Father so well, and trusted his love so deeply, that what the Father willed, Jesus loved. Dante followed in Jesus' steps as he learned to lay his will to rest in God's:

> Brother, our love has laid our wills to rest
> Making us long only for what is ours,
> And by no other thirst to be possessed.
>
> ...
>
> To his own will; and his will is our peace;
> This is the sea whereunto all things fare
> That it creates or nature furnishes.[10]

---

9   Piper, *Future Grace*, 390.
10 Dante, *Paradise*, trans. Sayers and Reynolds, Canto 3, 70–72, and 85–87, p. 75.

Freedom

We have the freedom to tell God "No." Many have given up. Many have failed. Some have experienced great sorrow and pain, but they finally could endure no more of it, and they fell and failed.

A few, like Polycarp,[11] would rather be burned alive than spurn the will of the Father. The will of the Father could conceive the redemption of the Cross of Jesus. The will of God could cover your sins with the perfections of your Savior and incorporate you into the body of Christ. The will of God could give you unspeakable joy, overflowing peace, and precious promises in this life, and Heaven in the next. Then could not that same will of God be trusted in your hour of trial? Loved more than life? Believed while you are in the world? Has not the will of the Father always been good, acceptable, and perfect (Cf. Romans 12:1–3.)?

Your sinful heart doubts the goodness of God, the wisdom of his will, the purpose of your sorrow, and the blessing of God over every event of your life. Your Dark Guest would convince you to deny the will of God so you could escape some trial here and now. But what of your life with God eternally after that fall?

In Heaven, the Savior could wipe away your tears, but it would take an aeon to knit together your broken heart. For after standing in Heaven's splendor and looking upon Jesus' glory, you will see his wounds with your own eyes and you will receive his welcoming love—the very wounds that won your salvation and forgiveness, will embrace you with never-ending mercy and love.

Standing there amid such grace, would you not long to offer your wounds to him who was wounded for you ("filling up what is lacking in the sufferings of Christ," Colossians 1:24)? Not as atonement for your sins, but as evidence that you lived your life in Christ, in him, to be like him in his death.

The wise among us would gladly choose the flames, the cross, and the pain to be more like him. Suffering and martyrdom are

---

11 *The Martyrdom of Polycarp*, Chapter 9, Sect. 3.

sure ways to be rid of that lying, thieving intruder, the Dark Guest, once and for all.

> Since therefore Christ suffered in the flesh, arm yourselves with the same way of thinking, for whoever has suffered in the flesh has ceased from sin. (1 Peter 4:1)

The Christian life can be lived. But how hard is that journey! Indwelling sin is a constant Guest driving your soul to turn from the love of God, the lordship of Christ, and the will of God. That power creates havoc, disloyalty, and life-breaking rebellion. But you can live the Christian life; you can mortify sin; you can choose holiness of life; you can love God with all you are and have. C.S. Lewis writes:

> There are only two kinds of people in the end: Those who say to God, "Thy will be done," and those to whom God says, "*Thy* will be done."[12]

A concluding quote from Sayers captures why her analysis of Dante moved me so to write this. She summarized the purpose of *The Divine Comedy*:

> To remove those living in this life from the state of misery and lead them to the state of felicity.[13]

A glorious goal for every believer is to live for Christ as Lord, fully convinced of the love of God, and uncompromisingly obedient to God's holy will. God grant that such lives may become quite ordinary.

---

12 Lewis, *The Great Divorce*, 69.
13 Sayers, *Introductory Papers on Dante*, Vol. 1, 129.

Resolutions

1. To know how sin held me captive when I yielded to it, and to renounce my captivity.
2. To believe that it is God's love that leads me to become a slave to God; and that being a slave to God is the greatest freedom I can have as a human being!
3. To be assured that nothing in all creation compares to the love of God; the love of God is the greatest expression of God's glory.
4. To confess with tears that I can become a Pharisee, keeping my holiness on the outside, following rules, and being controlling and damning of myself and of others.
5. To come to a point in my Christian life where I relinquish my will to God's will and to the Lordship of Christ as the most important and profound commitments of my life.
6. To experience the truths that God's love for me and my love for God are both crucial tests proving the validity of my saving faith.
7. To pray to the Father as my Savior prayed, "Not my will, but yours be done."
8. To pray to God that true holiness would be ordinary in my life every day until I go to Heaven.

Chapter Nine

A Humble Heart and a Holy Life

[Jesus Christ said,]"I have said these things to you, that in me you may have peace. In the world you will have tribulation. But take heart; I have overcome the world."
(John 16:33)

"We must go through many hardships to enter the kingdom of God." (Acts 14:22b)

"My little children, these things I write to you so that you may not sin." (1 John 2:1a)

Had I not passed by such a way, I should not have had this treasure; I should not have had means of joy in the City to which I approach.[1]

The Christian life can be lived to the glory of God. Some people have succeeded in being obedient to Jesus Christ. Paul said toward the end of his life, "I have kept the faith, I have finished the course," (2 Timothy 4:7c).

Scripture records examples of people who have mortified indwelling sin in their lives to some great extent. The apostle John praises

---

1   From Dante's *Convivio*, in Williams, *The Figure of Beatrice*, 229.

his Christian friends, "You have overcome the evil one" (1 John 2:13, cp. 2:14, 4:4, 5:4 and 5; then cp. John 16:33). Even though all sin is not mortified until we go to Heaven, some Christians win major battles against their grotesque sin, their public sin, and their debilitating and enslaving sin (cf. Romans 8:37; 1 Corinthians 15:57; and 1 John 5:4).

Battles are being won in this lifelong war against indwelling sin. People who succeed in this war may not be well-known Christians. But they are celebrated as victors in this war with sin. The most godly person is also going to be the most humble and the most God-dependent person you know. He will be the most broken and repentant and, therefore, the most victorious and fruitful. But those who finish well can all tell you the same truth: It will cost you to live a holy life; if you finish well.

Holiness by way of hardship

The Christian life is hard work. It requires discipline and self-control. It requires faith and obedience. It requires prayer and study. Moreover, it requires God's Spirit and the intercession of Jesus Christ in Heaven praying for you.

Even the most holy will fail in some very notable ways. It is clear from the Bible that you will fail in some areas and succeed in others (cf. Genesis 22:18 with Isaiah 53:6; Numbers 15:22; Acts 13:22; Romans 3:23; 2 Corinthians 2:9; and 1 Peter 2:20). But the God who redeemed you is committed to untying the ugly knot that has joined your new life of faith to the scandalous sins that captured your heart, destroyed your joy, soiled your witness, and disturbed your mind. Living the Christian life is most difficult for those who are the most successful at it. A.W. Pink writes:

> [The difficulty of Christian holiness is the greatest] unto those who are the most spiritual. Self-righteous Pharisees and self-satisfied Laodiceans are in no wise troubled over the matter. Antinomians cut the knot (instead of untying it) and deny all difficulty,

by asserting that the holiness of Christ is imputed to us. But those who realize God requires personal holiness, yet are conscious of their own filthiness, are deeply concerned thereupon.[2]

"Deeply concerned" about personal holiness would mean that the Christian thinks about holiness, strives for holiness, prays for more holiness, seeks the Spirit of holiness, and makes choices that will result in actual holiness of life.

To the contrary, self-righteous Pharisees seek external, outward, and superficial holiness. When examined at the heart-level, they are filled with filth (cf. Matthew 23:27). The Laodiceans (Revelation 3:14ff) are self-satisfied, lukewarm, and non-committal. They are neither hot nor cold. They are primarily concerned about themselves. They say, "I am rich, I have prospered, and I need nothing" (Revelation 3:17), but they are "wretched, pitiable, poor, blind, and naked."

Holiness does not come from contemplating sin.[3] You know that you cannot examine your sin and then devise some plan to combat it. Holiness comes from contemplating God, loving him, and then obeying his Word from the heart.

> Jesus answered him, "If anyone loves me, he will keep my word, and my Father will love him, and we will come to him and make our home with him. Whoever does not love me does not keep my words. And the word that you hear is not mine but the Father's who sent me." (John 14:23–24)

The holy life is lived in dependency upon God. You are destitute of holiness, but Christ does not leave you "in that awful estate."[4] Pink again writes:

---

2   Pink, *The Doctrine of Sanctification*, 44.

3   Ibid., 75.

4   Ibid., 141.

The aim of the Father's love and of the Son's grace was not only that we might have restored to us the life which we lost in Adam, but that we should have "life more abundantly"; that we should be brought back not merely to the position of servants— ... but be given the wondrous place of sons.[5]

Scriptural sanctification is neither the eradication of sin, the purification of the carnal [sinful] nature, nor even the partial putting to sleep of the 'flesh'; still less does it secure an exemption from the attacks and harassments of Satan.[6]

... and though it be true that at regeneration they receive from Christ, by the Spirit, a new and holy nature, like unto his; yet the old nature remains unchanged, unimproved. Yea, to them it seems that the carnal nature in them is steadily growing worse and worse, and more active and defiling every day they live. They are painfully conscious of the fact that sin not only remains in them, but that it pollutes their desires, thoughts, imaginations, and acts; and to prevent its uprisings they are quite powerless ....

A remarkable corroboration is found in the fact that the most godly and holy have been the very ones who most strongly affirmed their sinfulness and most loudly bewailed the same.[7]

---

5   Ibid., 141–142.
6   Ibid., 45.
7   Ibid., 63, 67.

The problem of sanctification

> Bear fruit in keeping with repentance. (Matthew 3:8)

The corrupting, unholy, atheistic stream of sin that floods every soul until Hell itself is filled, flows from the human heart. So, how can a sinful man be holy in the sight of God? How can one so vile and completely corrupt live a life of holiness and beauty before God? Some choices you made have created a connection within you to sins that are extremely difficult to break.

Sin captures and enslaves you. You didn't think that pornography would imprison you or that a little puff of pride would do you any harm. A little gossip couldn't hurt anyone. Who would know if you cheated on your income taxes? You didn't dream that having sex for fun would be dangerous. A heroin user doesn't begin his addiction by waking up one day and saying, "I think I'll begin using heroin today so that I can spend the rest of my life in and out of rehab." He starts with something he thinks he could control, and soon it is in control of every choice in his life. But it all begins so thoughtlessly. Sin makes you its slave.

Some sins are besetting. They require more than renunciation, outside support, and reliance upon spiritual disciplines. You can get yourself into a pit only God can get you out of (cf. Genesis 37:18ff, Joseph's pit). Some sins are so invasive, so controlling of your heart, so completely consuming that you are imprisoned and utterly dependent upon God's help alone to free you. Such liberation is not impossible, but these sins die hard, and they try to take you with them.

Underestimating sin's power is foolish. If you fight sin alone, you will be dragged to your own personal hell, there to live out the rest of your days under that sin's dominion and putrefaction.

> For no good tree bears bad fruit, nor again does a bad tree bear good fruit, for each tree is known

> by its own fruit. For figs are not gathered from thornbushes, nor are grapes picked from a bramble bush. The good person out of the good treasure of his heart produces good, and the evil person out of his evil treasure produces evil, for out of the abundance of the heart his mouth speaks. (Luke 6:43–45)

> But thanks be to God, that you who were once slaves of sin have become obedient from the heart to the standard of teaching to which you were committed. (Romans 6:17)

> What accord has Christ with Belial? Or what portion does a believer share with an unbeliever? (2 Corinthians 6:15)

> You therefore, beloved, knowing this beforehand, take care that you are not carried away with the error of lawless people and lose your own stability. (2 Peter 3:17)

> Outside are the dogs and sorcerers and the sexually immoral and murderers and idolaters, and everyone who loves and practices falsehood. (Revelation 22:15)

It is no surprise that Christians are few in number. Jesus said that would be the case:

> Enter by the narrow gate. For the gate is wide and the way is easy that leads to destruction, and those who enter by it are many. For the gate is narrow and the way is hard that leads to life, and those who find it are few. (Matthew 7:13–14)

If there is any rival to Jesus Christ in your life, you have not entered upon the narrow gate. If there is any love greater than your love for God, you are wandering on the broad plain. If there is any sin that you permit, excuse in yourself, blame on others, or upon God, then you have a terribly confused faith that may not be a saving faith at all.

The Christian life is lived by a person who is *transformed* by the power of the cross through the inner working of the Holy Spirit. A believer is *changed* to become like Jesus Christ. Sanctification is not making one's broken, rebellious, sinful self better. Sanctification is God making you holy (John 3:3, 7; Ephesians 2:15; and 1 Peter 1:3).

> ... for it is God who works in you, both to will and to work for his good pleasure. (Philippians 2:13)

John Owen writes about sanctification as a work of the Spirit:

> But this [mortification of sin] is the work of the Spirit; by him alone is it wrought. No other power can accomplish it. Mortification based on human strength, carried out with man-made schemes, always ends in self-righteousness. This is the essence and substance of all false religion in the world.[8]

Suffering, sorrow, and sanctification

In this life, sorrows, trials, and the discipline of God work to create, refine, and expand your holiness. If the sinful self, the Dark Guest is to be overcome, only Christ by his Spirit can accomplish this great work in the human heart. The Spirit of God uses trials and sorrows to test the quality of your faith and to make it more pure:

---

8 Owen, *Triumph over Temptation*, 193.

> And the ones on the rock are those who, when they hear the word, receive it with joy. But these have no root; they believe for a while, and in time of testing fall away. (Luke 8:13)
>
> Rejoice in hope, be patient in tribulation, be constant in prayer. (Romans 12:12)
>
> ... for you know that the testing of your faith produces steadfastness. (James 1:3)
>
> In this you rejoice, though now for a little while, if necessary, you have been grieved by various trials. (1 Peter 1:6)
>
> For this is a gracious thing, when, mindful of God, one endures sorrows while suffering unjustly. (1 Peter 2:19)
>
> ... then the Lord knows how to rescue the godly from trials, and to keep the unrighteous under punishment until the day of judgment. (2 Peter 2:9)

Sufferings and sorrows, trials and tribulations are sure to come:

> And [Jesus] said to his disciples, "Temptations to sin are sure to come, but woe to the one through whom they come!" (Luke 17:1)

The purpose of these trials and sorrows is to prove the quality of your faith:

> ... so that the tested genuineness of your faith—more precious than gold that perishes though it is tested by fire—may be found to result in praise and glory and honor at the revelation of Jesus Christ. (1 Peter 1:7)

Your difficulties come to you by a wise providence that directs your steps, provides for your welfare, controls the time and extent of your testing, limits the power of evil over you, permits there to be a beginning and an end to the seasons of testing, and creates in you a tested faith. When faced with these trials, you may want to run from them. Testing reveals how weak your faith is. Sorrows and trials are to be expected for every child of God. Suffering is normal:

> For it has been granted to you that for the sake of Christ you should not only believe in him but also suffer for his sake. (Philippians 1:29)

> Now I rejoice in my sufferings for your sake, and in my flesh I am filling up what is lacking in Christ's afflictions for the sake of his body, that is, the church. (Colossians 1:24)

Deny yourself

Your faith is weakest when you are most comfortable and at ease. Your faith is strongest when you are clinging to a plank in the ocean of trial. The ocean's power overshadows your sin, and the mighty roar of the storm silences sin's incessant beckonings. While you are adrift and lost, sin loses its power. The waves and the fierce winds of trial make your weaknesses abundantly clear. You are utterly incapable of saving yourself. Thank God for the plank that you can cling to that brings you ashore for brighter days ahead. A power is released in your sufferings to complete what is lacking in your faith. Jonathan Edwards writes:

> The great Christian duty is self-denial. This duty consists in two things: first, in denying worldly inclinations and its enjoyments, and second, in denying self-exultation and renouncing one's self-significance by being empty of self. Self-renunciation must be done freely, from the heart. Then a Christian will have evangelical [humility]. This last is the more difficult part of self-denial, although the two go together.[9]

Do you think it was without reason Noah was tested by the flood? Abraham was tested on Mount Moriah? Joseph was thrown into the pit? Job suffered the loss of everything? Daniel was thrown into the lion's den? Christ was tested in the desert? Or Paul was cast into prison and into the sea? Those accounts are what you should expect. The names, places and circumstances will differ, but you will face your mighty flood, your den of lions, and your loss of everything.

> More than that, we rejoice in our sufferings, knowing that suffering produces endurance. (Romans 5:3)

Trials reveal your motivations. One of the greatest proofs of the validity of the Christian faith is that those who proclaimed their faith in Christ often died for it. The apostles (from all accounts) were all killed. Their trials and sufferings make no sense if they were preaching a lie about a savior who faked his death. People don't suffer for a lie. People do give everything for their Savior who lived, who died, and who rose again from the dead.

In the holy pain of discipline, God mortifies your sin. God is far more concerned about your sin than about the pain of a disease, a desperate trial, or even your death. He is more focused on holiness than on healing, although he can and does heal. God is glorified by

---

9   Edwards, *Religious Affections*, 153.

his healing mercies.

And yes, God is still right when he allows people he loves to hurt, though no one said we would understand it all. "His ways are not our ways ...." I try not to argue with him when I am hurting. Job found that arguing with God was presumptuous and sinful:

> For he crushes me with a tempest
>   and multiplies my wounds without cause;
> he will not let me get my breath,
>   but fills me with bitterness.
> If it is a contest of strength, behold, he is mighty!
>   If it is a matter of justice, who can summon him?
> Though I am in the right, my own mouth would condemn me;
>   though I am blameless, he would prove me perverse.
> I am blameless; I regard not myself;
>   I loathe my life.
> (Job 9:17–21)

We sympathize with Job's cries and confusion. Those questions are as old as the Scriptures. We bury our friends and family members. We know people who have endured terrible trials. The sinful nature creates the fiction that we have some right to demand that God make it all okay. Your Dark Guest argues with God unceasingly. It demands that God do what the sinful self thinks is just and fair. That evil within argues with the Almighty and challenges him in what he does and in what he doesn't do. Sin doesn't submit to God, neither can it do so (cf. Romans 8:7). Bonhoeffer wrote about self-denial along this hard way of trials:

> To deny oneself is to be aware only of Christ and not more of self, to see only him who goes before and not more the road which is too hard for us. Once more, all that the self-denied can say is: he leads the way, keep close to him ... Only when we have become completely oblivious of self are we ready to bear the cross for his sake ... If Jesus had not so

graciously prepared us for this word, we should have found it unbearable ... To endure the cross is not a tragedy and it is the suffering which is the fruit of an exclusive allegiance to Jesus Christ.[10]

O Christ, you have denied yourself so that I can offer you my love, my obedience, my submission, my conformity to your will, my willingness to follow you everywhere and to do anything that you desire.

But I must die to my desires and live for yours. Even when praying about what I *should* do, I struggle. I yield to you, then I recant. I try to obey you, then I withdraw. I believe in you, then I doubt.

My hope, Dear Father, is that you would bring me to a branch in the road where one way is clearly your will, and another is not. So at that point of diversion, I may settle your supremacy in my life, at least for that point in time. Then later, when another decision must be made, you would help me then to choose again, to love you so much that I would only choose to follow you and to cling to your will above my own.

I cry to you: your will be done; your will be done; your will be done. Give me the love to choose you. By Jesus Christ I pray this. Amen.

Hope and victory

Indwelling sin will live within you until you die. How you

---

[10] Bonhoeffer, *The Cost of Discipleship*, 88.

silence the Dark Guest's voice, quiet its lusts, and put it to death, is the measure to which you will become a holy person. Sin and holiness are incompatible. God has left sin in you that you may come to him every hour and confess your great need for help and then claim Christ's victory over every sin.

God could have eradicated indwelling sin. He hasn't done it yet. Enduring and indwelling sin drives you constantly to Jesus to confess your sin and to claim his victory. His Holy Spirit demands that you take responsibility for your life and for all your choices. You know you are a sinner; and you know your Savior has defeated the power and presence of sin within you. You are no longer enslaved to any sin. Your prayers for help are not simply pleas for God to clean up your mess. They are prayers for victory.

The hope of this book is that you will do better, and that God, by his Holy Spirit, through the Word of God, for Jesus' sake, will make you holy. From *Paradise,* Christ's magnificence is reflected in the glory of Grace. All that he endured prepared him for this vision:

> Lift up thine eyes and look on me awhile
> See what I am; thou hast beheld such things
> As make thee mighty to endure my smile.[11]

---

11 Dante, *Paradise*, trans. Sayers and Reynolds, Canto 23, 46–48, p. 258.

Resolutions

1. To know that I can live the Christian life, but it will be costly for me.
2. To understand that the struggles to live a holy life are the greatest for those who are the most holy.
3. To believe that true holiness comes from contemplating God, not from examining my sin.
4. To be never deluded by underestimating sin's power in my life; because such miscalculation is evil and devastatingly foolish.
5. To expect testings and trials to come if I am to become more holy.
6. To prepare for coming trials by abiding in Christ and keeping in step with the Holy Spirit.
7. To refuse to argue with God when trials come, but to love him.
8. To have faith that no sin can defeat me, if my Savior gives me his victory over it.
9. To believe that, in Christ, I can sin less.

Appendix One

The War about Romans 7

The Westminster Confession of Faith, Chapter XII, Of Sanctification:

... (2)This sanctification is throughout, in the whole man; yet imperfect in this life, there abiding still some remnants of corruption in every part; whence ariseth a continual and irreconcilable war, the flesh lusting against the Spirit, and the Spirit against the flesh. (3) In which war, although the remaining corruption, for a time, may much prevail; yet, through the continual supply of strength from the sanctifying Spirit of Christ, the regenerate part doth overcome; and so, the saints grow in grace, perfecting holiness in the fear of God.

Calvinistic and Puritan authors and their modern successors, with few exceptions, held the view that the conflict with indwelling sin that Paul describes in Romans 7:13–25 is the experience of every believer in Christ. Calvin states, "until they are divested of mortal bodies, there is always sin."[1] Defending this historic view would have been unnecessary a century ago. But now there is a war being waged against the Augustinian and Reformed understanding of Romans 7. Leon Morris summarizes this view in his commentary on Romans 7:13–25:

---

1   Calvin, 3, 3, 15, *Institutes*, pp. 602–603.

> For surely this *is* the experience of the believer. No believer is completely sinless. He is still a sinner, no matter how much out of character his sin is. What happens when he does sin? He feels dreadful about it. Then why does he do it? He simply does not understand (Romans 7:15). In view of all that Christ has done for him and the resources Christ makes available for him, surely he should have resisted the temptation. He does not want to sin. He knows that. He knows that he ought not sin. But he is weak ("in the flesh"). Because he does not want to sin he can say with Paul, "I do what I do not want to do," (Romans 7:16)
>
> ... But he cannot deny his responsibility; his sin proceeds from what he is. He knows that he did it himself. But his regret is deep and genuine, and he cries, "O wretched man that I am!"[2]

The main thesis of this book is that indwelling sin is an ongoing problem for all Christians. The silence in many churches today about this pervasive problem with indwelling sin may relate to a recurring, frustrating, and presently intensifying debate about Paul's view of sin in the believer's life as he wrote Romans Chapter 7. This essay is to alert the reader to the scholarly debate over this portion of Romans and to suggest that the solution to the war over whether Paul was speaking of his life before he became a Christian or of his continuing struggle with sin after conversion, may rest not within the biblical text but on the presuppositions one brings to the text.

My habit in sermon preparation has been to go first to the biblical text, then to the grammars and lexicons, and then to the Reformed commentaries and theologians to get help for the passage

---

2   Morris, *The Epistle to the Romans*, 287–288.

I was studying. Those resources had proved reliable and personally beneficial on so many occasions that I regularly spun my exegetical orbit in those Calvinistic works.

Most Reformed commentators (with Herman N. Ridderbos and A. Hoekema as notable exceptions)[3] agree with the interpretation of Romans 7 that Paul was presenting his ongoing, present struggle with indwelling sin: that the sinful nature is still present in the Christian; and that its presence creates a difficult struggle for every believer.

Calvinistic scholars who hold this view are following Augustine's doctrine of indwelling sin and his reading of Romans 7. His analysis of the passage held sway for nearly fourteen centuries. Augustine was especially convinced by the use of the present tense in Romans 7 when Paul is describing his struggle with sin. This is to say that Paul was describing a continuing and current conflict within himself with sinful desires that moved him to cry out, "Wretched man that I am."[4] He was not describing his life before he met Christ, but his current situation.

The question is not so much did Calvinistic scholars follow

---

[3] Some scholars who hold to a pre-conversion reading of Romans 7:13ff: Paul Althaus, Jacob Arminus, Günther Bornkamm, Rudolf Bultmann, W.D. Davies, Karl Kertelge, Werner Kümmel, Douglas Moo, Rudolf Schnackenburg, James S. Stewart, Henry Clarence Thiessen, with many others.

Some scholars who hold to a post-conversion view: Augustine of Hippo, C.K. Barrett, Harold O.J. Brown, John Calvin, D.H. Campbell, D.A. Carson, C.E.B. Cranfield, C. James Dunn, Jonathan Edwards, Ronald Y.K. Fung, Everett K. Harrison, Carl F.H. Henry, Martin Luther, Philip Melanchthon, Leon Morris, Robert H. Mounce, John Murray, Anders Nygren, J.I. Packer, John Piper, J.C. Ryle, W.G.T. Shedd, C.H. Spurgeon, David Wells, and D. Wenham, with many others. I am more aware of writers in the second group than the first, and may have omitted several important names. These lists are not inclusive.

[4] Augustine of Hippo, *On Nature and Grace*, 55, 65, in Oden and Bray, *Ancient Christian Commentary on Scripture*, 196.

Augustine but did they (and Augustine) follow Paul?

Until the beginning of the 20th century, most New Testament commentaries sided with Augustine. A major shift occurred over the next 60 years. John Murray reported in his day (1959) a nearly equally divided house.[5] In a relatively short period of time, the Augustinian consensus was broken.

Contemporary scholars appear to be moving in even greater numbers away from Augustine and Calvin. Derek Thomas remarked almost in passing in his lecture on the history of "The Synod of Dort, Arminianism and Calvinism," that the pre-conversion view of Romans 7:13ff. has now become the dominant view among New Testament scholars.[6] Most recent scholarly commentaries on Romans (written after 1990) favor the view that the latter section of Romans 7 is about Paul's pre-Christian experience.

In this study we are adopting the traditional view that Christians are sinners saved by grace. We feel that this view most represents the teaching of the Bible and is most consistent with the creeds of Christianity. This is the most dominant view of the great luminaries of the Christian faith—Augustine; Dante; the early Reformers—Calvin and Luther, John Owen; the later Reformers Jonathan Edwards, George Whitefield; the French philosopher Blaise Pascal; the 19th-century English Baptist preacher C.H. Spurgeon; A.A. Hodge, C.H. Hodge, B.B. Warfield, of the late 19th and early 20th-century Princeton School; C.S. Lewis, the English apologist, author, and Medieval scholar; C.E.B. Cranfield; contemporary Puritans John Frame, C.J. Mahaney, J.I. Packer, and John Piper, and many others. Add to them the voices of some of the major commentaries on the books of Romans and Galatians (Luther, Calvin, Hodge, John Murray, Leon Morris, D.A. Carson and many others). This is no small weight of testimony in support of the view that Christians continue to experience the influence of indwelling sin until they enter into glory.[7] It would

---

5   Murray, *The Epistle to the Romans*, 256ff.
6   Thomas, "Theological Foundations: Dort, the Puritans and Hyper-Calvinism."
7   Ladd, *Introduction to the New Testament.*.

do us well to review Augustine's argument.

Augustine's argument, in brief, is that Paul uses the past tense to describe his former life in Judaism and the present tense when he speaks of his present life as a believer. Paul nowhere else uses the present tense to describe his past life. That distinction by Augustine between Paul's past and present life seems unassailable, and it should not be missed.

Those who hold that Paul's description of his inner war with sin is referring to his past life as a non-Christian Jew as a present-tense experience, are in an insurmountable difficulty. Exegetically, it is a huge leap to take the present tense and to thrust upon it past experiences.

The natural reading, following Augustine, is that Paul was using his life as an example of the ongoing struggle with indwelling sin that every believer experiences after he is saved.

By contrast, in Philippians 3 Paul describes his previous life using the past tense—a past life for which he grieves. His Phariseeism and zeal for the law did not cause him to cry out for mercy (cp. as he did at the end of Romans 7), it compelled him to arrest and to murder Christians. No more stark comparison can be made between Paul in the past wanting to arrest and even murder believers and Paul in the present pleading with God for mercy and victory over his sin. In Romans 7 Paul cries out for help, not vengeance. The difference could not be clearer.

The accumulated injunctions for Christians to stop sinning throughout the New Testament are the strongest commentary about our continuing struggle with indwelling sin. Dozens of Scriptures call for Christians to stop sinning. For example, in Ephesians 5:1–14, Paul speaks to Christians against immorality, impurity, covetousness, filthiness, foolish talk, crude joking, impurity, and unfruitful works of darkness. These commands touch a broad span of sins, dealing with everything from foolishness to immorality. Paul wrote the correctives because Christians he knew were sinning (just like today) and Paul spoke to them directly and with authority to stop sinning.

In this discussion about Romans 7, it is not compelling to me that Augustine supports the view we are espousing. Augustine could be wrong. Evidence from church fathers is interesting, but not persuasive, even if it supports one's view. The fathers wander from orthodoxy in many ways and the correctives of many centuries of fights about core doctrines are evidence that in that formative period many were misled, confused, or flat wrong.[8]

A more interesting question would be: Did Augustine follow the intention of Paul? Augustine bears authority only because he was Paulist (a follower of *Paul*, rather than as a Calvinist who is a follower of *Calvin*). Augustine was not a Calvinist. Paul was not an Augustinian. It works the other way around. The same is true of Calvin, or Spurgeon, or Warfield, or Lloyd-Jones, or Packer, or Sproul. Paul wasn't a Calvinist or an Augustinian. Calvin and Augustine were Paulists.

There appears to be some connection between those who espouse the view that Romans 7:13–25 is pre-Christian with the Arminian and Pelagian views of human sin. A quick survey of the scholars will quickly show almost uniform alignment of the Calvinists with Augustine, and the Arminians with modern scholars. Theology ought not to drive one's view of Scripture. Scripture ought rather to drive one's theology.

Turning to the practical: For me it is immensely liberating to say, "I struggle with about every sin there is. I am shocked at what I can think up to do. But by God's grace and the help of the Spirit of God, I don't do the stuff I can dream up." I am (as a friend quips) "four minutes from any sin." But I am victorious in Christ over all of them. Thanks be to God.

So can I sin? Yes, you bet. But do I sin? Sometimes, yes. But one ought to sin less in scandalous ways, or ways that publicly, overtly dishonor the Christian faith.

The war with indwelling sin is a life-long struggle. But this is a struggle that scholars I have read and trusted for so many other insights, doctrines, and Christian practices, their help here is all the

---

8 Brown, *Heresies*.

more encouraging and convincing.

My experience, from one man's life, is that this struggle with indwelling sin is a very strong and encouraging evidence of true and saving faith. A.W. Pink writes this:

> Scriptural sanctification is neither the eradication of sin, the purification of the carnal nature, nor even the partial putting to sleep of the 'flesh'; still less does it secure an exemption from the attacks and harassments of Satan.
>
> ... It is perfectly plain to any simple soul that a 'pure heart' cannot signify one from which all sin has been removed, nor can their language possibly by made to square with the utopian theory that the carnal nature is eradicated from any believer in this life.[9]

Knox Chamblin captures the scope of this lifelong struggle:

> There is a healthy realism about Romans 7:14–25. The Christian is granted new understanding both of God's law (7:16, 22–23) and of Sin's designs. Moreover, with growth in holiness comes a deeper awareness of the powerlessness of the self. The ones most acutely aware of the struggle depicted here are not the spiritually infantile but the spiritually mature. The more one experiences the presence of Christ and the power of the Spirit, the more one recognizes the inadequacy of the autonomous self. [Quoting C.E.B. Cranfield] 'The man in whom the power of sin is really being seriously and resolutely challenged, in him the power of sin is clearly seen. The more he is renewed by God's Spirit, the more sensitive he

---

9   Pink, *The Doctrine of Sanctification*, 45, 67–68.

> becomes to the continuing power of sin over his life and the fact that even his very best activities are marred by the egotism still entrenched within him.' Thus with ever more fervent longing, he utters the cry of 7:24–25a ["O Wretched Man that I am!"].[10]

If my reading of Paul is wrong—if sin is not an issue within you as a believer, because of Christ's victory, or the Holy Spirit's presence, or the power of the Word of God—then we have little in common with Paul's anguish about the old man and a shared warfare with indwelling sin. Such language as "O Wretched Man" would make no sense to at all.

My view is that this conflict with indwelling sin is real, potentially devastating to our spiritual growth and fruitfulness, and continuous until we die. Today after 1,400 years of consensus, that Augustinian and (later) Reformed understanding of Paul in Romans 7 is being repudiated.

But to depart from Paul at this point unravels the New Testament understanding of sin, salvation, and the Savior. If indwelling sin is no longer present or poses little challenge within the life of the believer, would not holiness be much more common in our experience and in Christians' lives generally?

Every believer should study the questions about indwelling sin found in Romans 7. Commentaries could be of use after you have a good grasp of the argument in Romans. Read all you can, but ultimately the questions are going to be:

> "What is the most natural reading of the text of Romans 7 about the nature of indwelling sin?" And then,

> "How shall I live for Christ based upon that reality?"

---

10 Chamblin, *Paul and the Self*, 176.

Appendix Two

The Question of Meaning

Nature says, "I am not God." [1]

Is there a relationship between the loss of meaning and the rise of selfishness? Is there a link between the disconnection from our Creator and meaning that is attached to his majesty and Godhood, and the rise of self-idolatry, self-aggrandizement, and self-deception? The tide of selfishness is washing over every home, business, institution, political party, church, and person. Where did this deluge of selfishness come from?

The roots of this for our modern time came from the period of the French Revolution and the founding of America. A new approach to thinking about the world gave rise to a radical new philosophical underpinning for all of modern science—the way that modern man perceived the world. Everything changed about the way questions were asked, and about the reach of our philosophical and scientific inquiry. In science, theology, ethics, theories of education, the view of humanity's purpose and value, the greatest question of all is, "What is the meaning of life?"

C.S. Lewis and Owen Barfield

C.S. Lewis did more to put the meaning question back on the table for thoughtful discussion than any other modern writer. It was the meaning questions that drove him to Christianity. He saw the God

---

1   Calvin, *Institutes*, 1, 14, 18, p. 177.

questions being addressed in ancient myths in almost every culture. He understood the myths as longings and unanswered questions of people yearning to know who they were and how they should live and die. The questions of the meaning of human life, of love, of God, went far beyond drops in a test tube or calculating the rate of deterioration of an isotope. Through his vast learning, not despite it, Lewis was looking for God. And he wasn't alone.

Lewis was part of a group of thinkers and writers called the "Inklings."[2] Owen Barfield was a member of this group. Barfield was a writer, scholar, reviewer, critic, lawyer, philosopher, and light for his day. He was a friend of Lewis and his musings about his friend's life and thoughts were collected in a celebrated book.[3] Barfield was trustee of the C.S. Lewis estate.

Barfield also wrote philosophical and analytical articles, longer essays, and books. His essay "The Rediscovery of Meaning" caused quite a stir in 1961 when it was first published in the *Saturday Evening Post*.[4] Its main point is still brilliantly relevant today. Barfield wrote his 1961 article about Auguste Comte's (1798–1857) essay that challenged the usefulness of meaning questions for scientific inquiry.

Comte sent out his salvo against meaning with the publication of his *Plan of Scientific Studies Necessary for the Reorganiza-*

---

[2] The "Inklings" included: C.S. Lewis, Owen Barfield, Charles Williams, Christopher Tolkein, Charles Williams, Warren Lewis, Roger Lancelyn Green, Adam Fox, Hugo Dyson, Robert Havard, J.A.W. Bennett, Lord David Cecil, Nevill Coghill and sometimes Percy Bates, Charles Leslie Wrenn, Colin Hardie, J.R.R. Tolkein, John Wain, R.B. McCallum, Gervase Mathew, C.E. Stevens, and E.R. Eddison. Dorothy L. Sayers is often cited as a member though she did not attend, but was a friend of several in the group.

[3] Barfield, *Owen Barfield on C. S. Lewis*.

[4] Barfield, "The Rediscovery of Meaning," *Saturday Evening Post*, January 7, 1961: 36–37, 61, and 64–65; later republished in Barfield, *The Rediscovery of Meaning, and Other Essays*.

*tion of Society*⁵. This seminal work created the framework for a new approach to science based solely on observation and the analysis of data separated from any inference to the questions of meaning.

The separation of science from God was an idea that was generally benign at first: The concern then was that science not be constrained by religious dogma, if it be about whether our galaxy is heliocentric or geocentric, or the age of the Earth, or the date of the creation of the universe—those questions had been biased by religious dogma. Science had come to a point where they wanted to separate facts from religion. Comte, quite fairly, wanted there to be free discussion of matters of science unencumbered by the inferential questions of the philosophers and theologians. At the beginning, the separation of meaning questions from science freed the scientist from the arms of the church.

Comte's philosophy was called *positivism*. Science, by this method, must be pure, positivistic in its approach to the subject being studied, and indifferent to larger questions about causality, purpose, and values. Pure science was to discover whatever it discovered; no deductions were to be drawn except to other matters of fact. The larger subject of meaning was beyond the scope and possibility of the positivists as they constructed this new approach to scientific inquiry. For about 100 years (until 1900), this approach continued to gain support, and some remarkable scientific discoveries were made. Keeping the issue of the *meaning* of the discoveries outside of the scientific investigations became standard practice for experimental scientists.

Meaninglessness and selfishness

By the beginning of the 19th century, this polite separation became a mandate. Comte called for the formal separation of the meaning questions. What had been adopted as a useful approach to scientific questions, leaving theology and philosophical questions aside, became much more than a method, it became a dogma.

---

5   Comte, *Plan de travaux scientifiques nécessaries pour réorganizer la société.*

What had been a useful mechanism for science to focus on the issues of fact and observation became an unbridgeable barrier for the pursuit of the metaphysical questions of meaning. There was established a formal and intentional separation of the meaning questions from the science questions. Barfield writes:

> Thus, in investigating the phenomena of nature, exclusive emphasis on physical causes and effects involves a corresponding inattention to their meaning. And it was just this exclusive emphasis which came into fashion about three hundred years ago. What happened later, in the nineteenth century, was that a *habit* of inattention (sometimes explicit but more often implicit) that scientific attention to the meaning, as distinct from the causes of phenomena, as impossible—even if (which was considerably improbable) there was anything to attend to. The meaning of a process is the inner being which the process expresses. The denial of any such inner being to the processes of nature leads inevitably to the denial of it in man himself … it is implicit in positivism that man can never really know anything about his specifically human self—his own inner being—any more than he can ever really know anything about the meaning of the world of nature by which he is surrounded.[6]

Note the progression. Meaning questions were first set aside, then ignored, then forbidden (by Comte), and finally, they were ruled impossible (by the later positivists). In a span of 300 years, meaning was ruled by science as meaningless. It wasn't as if the meaning questions were ruled out by honest debate, by deduction

---

6 Barfield, *The Rediscovery of Meaning, and Other Essays*, "The Rediscovery of Meaning," 12.

from evidence, from consensus from the scientists. Meaning was declared impossible through an adopted philosophical belief-system imposed over time upon the scientific community.

Our focus in this is that the meaning questions are not benign. They are profound, pressing, and inescapable questions that every human being asks and answers for himself in some way. People persist in asking meaning questions. They appear to be unavoidable despite the modern prejudice against them.

Christianity and meaning

A central thesis of Christianity is that meaning is everywhere, in every aspect of creation, and in every event. Christians affirm that God is sovereign over every action of men, even the vilest of men, that God has placed meaning in everything, and that this God-placed meaning is comprehensible to people. Every fact speaks of God. The message of meaning is humbling to people. We are not in control of the universe. We can't understand everything. We are not in charge of the actions of others and we don't always get what we want. Our lives are marred with sin and suffering is common to everyone. The claim of God demands an answer.

Revealed faith asserts that God exists and that he reveals himself in terms people can understand in everything he has made.

> For what can be known about God is plain to them,
> because God has shown it to them. (Romans 1:18)

God made things to tell us about his nature, his goodness, his genius, his wisdom, and his majesty. There is order in the created world because the God who made everything is orderly. Chaos or randomness can be a principle employed by an artist creating interesting modern art, but chaos can never make life from stardust. Randomness cannot make life out of nothing, even given billions and billions of years. Chaos cannot create order.

The positivists demand you ask only *What?*, *How?*, *Where?*, and

When? But never *Why?* (in the cosmological sense). So if meaning is laced throughout everything in the universe and it all declares the glory of God, then meaninglessness is a lie. But in our modern world-system meaninglessness is a lie that must be propagated, believed, evangelized, and canonized, and those who reject it must be punished.

If dark matter exists, we can find meaning in that assertion of fact that points to a glorious and powerful God who made it—even in the shadowy, imprecise, and tentative observations of science that we now have about this strange substance that fills most of the mass of the universe. Dark matter, as all things, says something about God.

We study a phenomenon and sit back in our chairs knowing less than when we began to study. Because we learned so very much, so many new things, our "not knowing" is now expanded by our "knowing."

Within the cells of a leaf we can see a universe of molecule-sized chemical machines of incredible complexity on an impossibly tiny scale. A bird's song is a symphony. A beam of light is so complex that it empties the human mind of the presumption that we know much about the world—a particle traveling at the speed of light is impossible; it must have infinite mass to travel so fast, according to Einstein; and it is a wave and a particle simultaneously! Impossible! The Monarch butterfly migrates thousands of miles to the same location in Mexico every few years and we do not know how it happens. Our knowing opens windows onto what we do not know.

What do we know? How much more is there to learn? The Creator has fashioned the universe in God-sized proportions. Much of it is knowable. He has etched his wisdom in incredible details of depth, intricacies, and complexities that only God could have created by his mind and fashioned by his own hand.

Why attack meaning?

Modern positivists, the "logical positivists," assert that communication between people is impossible. What could we know? What could be said? Could any statement be meaningful? If meaning is impossible, language is impossible as well.

This dead-end philosophy reminded Barfield of a quote from C.S. Lewis reflecting on what the positivists really mean—namely, that all human language, by their reading, is "almost nobody making linguistic mistakes about almost nothing."[7]

Nothing is more absurd than people trying to remove all meaning from the world. But as you will see, this removal of meaning had a grander purpose.

Religion exists, by the positivist's reading, as a mistaken conclusion reached by people who have wrongly understood the facts of science and history. Positivists believe any view of meaning in the world can be attributed only to the imagination of the observer. Believers have imbued meaning into observations that positivists reduce to facts, data points, or calculations, and they are therefore, from the positivists' point of view, making linguistic errors.

The positivists hold that any conclusions or deductions beyond counting, measuring, and comparing within the natural realm are, *ipso facto*, meaningless. While the believers see what God has made and give him glory for it all, those claims are summarily rejected as erroneous or mythological by the positivists. When it is suggested that meaning does exist, the positivists object that those who saw connections with the meaning of life or the Creator have really just misunderstood what they have seen.

So God becomes a mistake. The universe only has facts. Religious faith is pushed neatly aside. Faith is an error in language. And all because positivists declared that meaning is impossible.

Now we can see how we got where we are today. People have been taken captive by this dogma. Before the positivist dogma was established so broadly in the scientific and philosophical communities, people saw unity in the incredible complexity of nature (e.g., shared life on earth in divergent habitats, the beauty and wonder of reproduction, the balance and breadth of design in living creatures and physical systems, and interdependency of environmental systems

---

7   Ibid., 13.

that support great diversity and complexity, etc.). These questions and answers were of a cosmological nature that caused people to confront the question of meaning, and more important, the question of God.

Selfishness is disrupted by the very thought of God. If I am selfish (and I am), then the personal presence of God revealing his wisdom and power everywhere, and the possibility that this marvelously complex and sovereign power so convincingly made his presence known in all he has made, will have a restraining effect on my life. It might even cause me to ask a meaningful question about what happens to me when I die. But I am getting ahead of the argument.

By freeing the soul from questions of meaning, the self is cut off from ultimate questions. By the death of meaning, selfishness is excused from any moral accountability to the Creator. Apart from meaning, the self can do as it wants. It can think what it will. The self is, therefore, the measure of every value.

Selfish people live in an internal war with meaning. Meaninglessness supports and defends selfishness. Without meaning, you could live solely for yourself. Logically, you could not sustain a philosophy of selfishness if you were convinced that Almighty God exists.

If God and meaning exist, you ought to live carefully and responsibly for other people and for God. Barfield writes:

> It remains to be considered whether the future of scientific man must inevitably continue in the same direction, so that he becomes more and more a mere onlooker, measuring with greater and greater precision and manipulating more and more cleverly an earth to which he grows spiritually more and more a stranger. His detachment has enabled him to describe, weigh, and measure the processes of nature and to a large extent to control them; but the price he has paid has been the loss of his grasp on any meaning in either nature or himself.[8]

---

8   Ibid., 18.

Selfish people live in a succession of decisions that do not matter in the company of people who do not matter. They are an unseen ripple in a pond that doesn't exist. Meaning for them has been given up without a whimper of protest.

But everything, despite the protests of the selfish, is significant of God. Not all things equally so, but all things extensively bear evidence of the Creator's hand, his wisdom, his mercy, his might, his justice, and his redeeming love. All things have meaning.

The positivists can never ask *"Why?"* Every created thing, every circumstance, every emotion, and every need, bring your hearts, minds, and wills to the larger questions of meaning that we long to ask—the questions of *Why?* and *Who am I?*

Everyone can see that the heavens declare the glory of God (Psalm 19; Romans 1). The vastness of space, the depths of the sea, and the marvels of life everywhere, all give testimony to the awesome power and majesty of a marvelously intelligent God. They also speak with abundant clarity to the hearts of those who can take it all in. It means something wonderful: Nothing God has made is meaningless; everything God has done brings him glory; therefore, the world and our lives have significance in him.

Scripture Index

Genesis
2:7 — 104
3 — 44
12:2 — 46
22:18 — 144
37:18ff — 147
38 — 63

Exodus
20:17 — 54

Leviticus
13 and 14 — 98

Numbers
15:22 — 144

Deuteronomy
5:21 — 54
13:3 — 69

Joshua
1:8 — 90
7:11 and 20 — 115

1 Samuel
16:7 — 88
25:37 — 25

2 Samuel
11 and 12 — 63, 115

2 Chronicles
5:13 — 47
7:13 — 47

Job
9:17–21 — 153
41:24 — 25

Psalm
1 — 90
10:3 — 58
18:23 — xv
25:4ff — 137
32 — 43, 115
37:11 — 89
51 — 43, 115
63:4 — 46
86:12 — 20
106:1 — 47
107:1 — 47
118:1 — 47
119 — 90
136:1 — 47
139:7 — xvii, 21
140:8 — 58
145:2 — 46
145:9 — 15, 16 47

Proverbs
5:22–23 — 33, 56
29:1 — 47

Isaiah
5:20–21 — 103
6:3 — 97
44:9–20 — 19
50:10 — 122
53:6 — 144
55:8 — 6
64:6 — 117

Jeremiah
33:11 — 47

Ezekiel
11:19, 36:26 — 25

Daniel
3:29 — 5

Hosea
5:4 — 56

Haggai
2:19 — 46

Matthew
3:8 — 126, 147
5:5 — 89
5:5–7 — 46
7:13 — 6
7:13–14 — 148
7:16, 20 — 92
7:22–23 — 22
15:19 — 92

16:24–26	109	**Acts**		7:20	40
18:8	18	3:19	114	7:23	17, 79, 129
18:8–9	49	5:1–11	116	8:1	134
18:13	77	5:41	48	8:7	153
23:27	145	13:13	48	8:10	40
24:24	80	13:22	144	8:13	82, 91
		14:17	47	8:14	71
Mark		14:19	48	8:15	106
4:19	58	14:22b	143	8:16	106
7:21–23	117	15:9	74	8:29	83
		21:10–14	48	8:35–39	131
Luke		26:20	114	8:37	144
5:32	10, 114, 126			8:38–39	136
6:43–45	148	**Romans**		12:1–3	140
7:50	74	1:5	74	12:12	150
8:13	150	1:18	169	13:14	59
9:23	109	1:25	47	14:8	137
13:3	111, 114	2:8	17	14:23	40
13:5	114	3:11	36	15:7	37
16:15	21	3:23	47, 144		
17:1	150	4:5	117	**1 Corinthians**	
17:4	114	5:3	152	2:16	83
18:13	116	5:5	20, 43	5:2	40
19:10	10	5:8	38	6:9–11	84
22:31	80, 84	6:1ff	40, 123	6:18	40
22:42	55, 139	6:4	36, 37, 38	9:7	74
23:39ff	135	6:5	133	10:13	42, 125
24:46–27	126	6:6	17, 34	10:31	20
24:47	114	6:6a	41	11:28	98
		6:8	34	13:8	27
John		6:11	18, 34	15:22	134
3:3, 7	149	6:13	40	15:57	144
3:16	38	6:13–14	137		
5:19	136	6:17	148	**2 Corinthians**	
5:42	136	6:17–18	35	2:9	144
7:38	92	6:22	130	3:3	25
8:44	58	7	17, 54	3:18	83, 117
14:15	108, 135	7:7	54	4:16b	16
14:23–24	145	7:12	57	5:14–15	1, 137
15:5	136	7:13	57	6:15	148
17:9	80	7:13–25	157	7:1	xiv
17:17b	117	7:17	40, 41	7:9	115

7:10	117	1:29	151	4:7	75
10:3	79	2:1–10	36	4:7c	143
10:3f	74	2:3	89	4:16	79
11:21	115	2:5	83		
12:21	112	2:12–13	122	**Titus**	
13:5	98, 105	2:13	134, 149	1:15	43
		2:25	74		
Galatians		3:10	37	**Philemon**	
2:16	57	3:12	95	1:2	74
2:20	19, 39, 73	3:13	80, 124		
4:6	106	4:13	136	**Hebrews**	
5:16	91			2:11	123
5:17	59	**Colossians**		3:13	27
5:24	59	1:5	91	4:12	27
5:25	92	1:24	140, 151	4:15	79, 96
6:17	48	3:5	82	6:1	114
		3:9	82	6:6	113
Ephesians		3:10	16	6:11–12	122
1:13	91			6:14	46
2:1–2	38	**1 Thessalonians**		7:25	80
2:8	8, 74	4:1	10, 25, 135	11:6	74
2:11–22	30	5:8	75	11:29	43
2:15	149	5:10	38	12:1	26
3:17	74			13:6	49
3:19f	21	**2 Thessalonians**		13:12	134
4:6	40	2:11–12	90		
4:13	83			**James**	
4:22	59	**1 Timothy**		1:3	150
4:24	xiv, 17, 125	1:15	40	1:18	91
5:1–2	108	1:18	74, 75	1:21	90
5:1–14	161	4:4–5	91	3:13	90
5:2	37	5:20	40	3:14 and 16	16
5:3	xvi	6:12	74, 75	4:1	95
5:23	37	6:19	41	4:6	89
5:25	37	6:20	47	4:8	40
5:29	37				
6:6	138	**2 Timothy**		**1 Peter**	
6:11	13, 80	2:3	74	1:3	149
6:12	74	2:11	19, 34	1:4–5	106
		2:15	91	1:6	150
Philippians		2:25	114	1:7	151
1:27	75	3:5	24	1:14–16	35

1:16	xiv	**1 John**		**Revelation**	
1:22	21	2:1a	143	2:5	114
2:19		2:5	65, 136	3:14ff	
2:20	144	2:13	144	3:17	145
4:1	48, 141	2:15–16	60, 61	3:19	115
5:5	89	2:16–17	65	4:8	97
5:5–6	90	2:17	68	7:14	134
		2:29	40	21:8	74
2 Peter		3:2	85, 124	22:15	148
1	113, 134	4:10	135		
1:3	38	4:19	21		
1:4	5	5:4	74, 144		
2:9	150	5:13	40, 106		
3:3	59				
3:9	114, 126	**Jude**			
3:11	xiv	16	59		
3:17	148				

Bibliography

Akin, Daniel L., David P. Nelson, and Peter R. Shemm, Jr., *A Theology for the Church*. Nashville: B&H Publishing Group, 2007.

Augustine of Hippo, *Confessions*, translated by F.J. Sheed. Indianapolis: Hackett, 1992.

Augustine, *Confessions and Enchiridion, Library of Christian Classics*, Vol. VII. Philadelphia: Westminster Press, 1955 (uncopyrighted edition).

Saint Augustine, Bishop of Hippo, *On Christian Teaching*. Oxford: Oxford University Press, 1997.

Barfield, Owen, *Owen Barfield on C.S. Lewis*, edited by G.B. Tennyson. London: The Barfield Press, 2006.

———."The Rediscovery of Meaning," *Saturday Evening Post* (January 7, 1961) 36–7, 61, and 64–65.

———.*The Rediscovery of Meaning and Other Essays*. Middletown, CT: Wesleyan University Press, 1977.

Barrett, C.K., *The Epistle to the Romans*. London: A & C Black, 1962.

Baxter, Richard, *Watch your Walk: Ministering from a Heart of Integrity (The Reformed Pastor)*, edited by James M. Houston. Colorado Springs: Victor – Cook, 1985.

Bennett, Arthur, editor, *The Valley of Vision: A Collection of Puritan Prayers and Devotions*. Carlisle, PA: Banner of Truth Trust, 1975.

Bonhoeffer, Dietrich, *The Cost of Discipleship {Nachfolge}*, translated by by R.H. Fuller and Irmgard Booth. New York: Touchstone, 1937 (German), 1959 (English).

Bridges, Jerry, *The Discipline of Grace*. Colorado Springs: NavPress, 1991.

———.*Transforming Grace: Living Confidently in God's Unfailing Love*. Colorado Springs: NavPress, 1991.

Brown, Harold O.J., *Heresies: The Image of Christ in the Mirror of Heresy and Orthodoxy from the Apostles to the Present*. New York: Doubleday, 1984.

Bunyan, John, *Pilgrim's Progress*. London: Dalziel Brothers, 1880.

Calvin, John, *The Institutes of the Christian Religion* (The Library of Christian Classics, Vol. XX), translated by Ford Lewis Battles, edited by John T. McNeill. Philadelphia: Westminster, 1960.

Candlish, Robert S., *A Commentary of 1 John*. Carlisle, PA: Banner of Truth Trust, 1993 (a reprint of the 1877 Edinburgh: A & C Black edition).

Carnell, Edward John, *The Burden of Søren Kierkegaard*. Grand Rapids: Eerdmans, 1956.

Carson, D. A., *Exegetical Fallacies*. Grand Rapids: Baker, 1996.

———.*The Gagging of God: Christianity Confronts Pluralism.* Grand Rapids: Zondervan, 1996.

Chamblin, J. Knox, *Paul and the Self: Apostolic Teaching for Personal Wholeness*. Grand Rapids: Baker Books, 1993.

Collins, Jim, *Good to Great*. New York: HarperCollins, 2001.

Comte, Auguste, *Plan de travaux scientifiques nécessaries pour réorganizer la société*. Paris: Suite des travaux ayant pour objet de fonder le système industriel, DU CONTRAT SOCIAL, par Saint-Simon, 1822.

Dante Alighieri, *The Divine Comedy of Dante Alighieri: Hell, Purgatory, Paradise*, The Harvard Classics, Vol. XX, translated by Henry F. Cary, edited by Charles W. Eliot. New York: P. F. Collier, 1909–14.

———. *Inferno*, translated by Henry Wadsworth Longfellow, edited with preface by Matthew Pearl. New York: The Modern Library, 2003 (a reprint of the 1867 Leipzig: Bernhard Tauchnitz edition).

———.*The Comedy of Dante Alighieri*, Cantica I, *Hell (L'Inferno)*, translated by Dorothy L. Sayers. London: Penguin, 1949.

———.*The Comedy of Dante Alighieri*, Cantica II, *Purgatory (Il Purgatorio)*, translated by Dorothy L. Sayers. London: Penguin, 1955.

———.*The Comedy of Dante Alighieri*, Cantica III, *Paradise* (*Il Paradiso*), translated by Dorothy L. Sayers and Barbara Reynolds. London: Penguin, 1962.

Denney, James, *The Death of Christ*, edited by R.V.G. Tasker. London: Tyndale, 1951.

Edwards, Jonathan, *Charity and Its Fruits*. New York: Robert Carter and Brothers, 1854.

———. "Edwards, Jon. Letter 1741 to a young lady residing in Smithfield, Conn.," *God's Call to Young People*, edited by Don Kistler. Morgan, PA: Soli Deo Gloria Press, 2001.

———. *The Religious Affections*. Carlisle, PA: Banner of Truth Trust, 1994 (reprint of the 1746 Boston: S. Kneeland and T. Green edition).

———. *The Works of Jonathan Edwards*, Vol. 1. Carlisle, PA: Banner of Truth Trust, 1998.

Eliot, T.S., "Notes Toward the Definition of Culture," *Christianity and Culture: The Idea of a Christian Society AND Notes Toward the Definition of Culture*. San Diego: Harcourt, 1976.

Fletcher, Joseph F., *Situation Ethics*. Louisville: Westminster John Knox, 1966.

Foster, Richard, *Prayer: Finding the Heart's True Home*. New York: HarperCollins, 1992.

Harrison, Everett F., in *The Expositor's Bible Commentary*: Vol. 10, *Romans*, edited by Frank E. Gaebelein. Grand Rapids: Zondervan, 1976.

Henry, Carl F.H., *God, Revelation and Authority.* Wheaton: Crossway, 1999.

Hodge, A.A., *The Confession of Faith.* Edinburgh: Banner of Truth Trust, 1958.

Kreeft, Peter, *C.S. Lewis for the Third Millennium: Six Essays on The Abolition of Man.* San Francisco: Ignatius, 1994.

———. *Back to Virtue: Traditional Moral Wisdom for Modern Moral Confusion.* San Francisco: Ignatius, 1992.

Ladd, G.E., *Introduction to the New Testament.* Grand Rapids: Eerdmans, 1993.

Lewis, C.S., *The Great Divorce.* New York: Macmillan, 1958.

———. *Present Concerns*, edited by Walter Hooper. London: Harvest, 1986.

———. *The Screwtape Letters: With Screwtape Proposes a Toast.* San Francisco: HarperSanFrancisco, 1996.

———. *Studies in Words.* Cambridge: Cambridge University Press, 1960.

Lloyd-Jones, D.M., *Darkness and Light.* Grand Rapids: Baker, 1982.

Luther, Martin, *The Bondage of the Will*, translated by J.I. Packer and O.R. Johnston. Grand Rapids: Fleming H. Revell, 1957.

———. *Lectures on Romans*, edited by Wilhelm Pauck. Philadelphia: Westminster, 1961.

Mahaney, C.J., *Humility: True Greatness*. Colorado Springs: Multnomah, 2005.

Manning, Brennan, *The Signature of Jesus: On the Pages of Our Lives*. Portland, OR: Multnomah, 1992.

Marshall, Walter, *The Gospel Mystery of Sanctification*. Eugene, OR: Wipf & Stock, 2005.

The Martyrdom of Polycarp, translated by Alexander Roberts and James Donaldson, from *Ante-Nicene Fathers*, Vol. 1., edited by Alexander Roberts, James Donaldson, and A. Cleveland Coxe. Buffalo, NY: Christian Literature, 1885.

Miller, C. John, *The Heart of a Servant Leader: Letters from Jack Miller*, edited by Barbara Miller Juliani. Phillipsburg, NJ: P & R, 2004.

Morris, Leon, *The Apostolic Preaching of the Cross*. London: Tyndale, 1955.

———. *The Cross in the New Testament*. Grand Rapids: Eerdmans, 1965.

———. *The Epistle to the Romans*. Grand Rapids and Cambridge: Eerdmans, 1988.

Mounce, Robert H., *The New American Commentary*, Vol. 27, *Romans*, edited by E. Ray Clendenen. Nashville: Broadman and Holman, 1995.

Murray, John, *The Epistle to the Romans: The English Text with Introduction,* Exposition and Notes. Grand Rapids: Eerdmans, 1959.

Oden, Thomas C. and Gerald L. Bray, editors, *Ancient Christian Commentary on Scripture:* New Testament, VI, *Romans*. Downers Grove, IL: InterVarsity, 1998.

Owen, John, *The Holy Spirit*, edited by R.J.K. Law. Carlisle, PA, The Banner of Truth Trust, 1998.

———.*Overcoming Sin and Temptation*, edited by Kelly M. Kapic and Justin Taylor. Wheaton: Crossway, 2006.

———.*Triumph Over Temptation: Pursuing a Life of Purity* [*Sin and Temptation*, 1983], introduction by J.I. Packer, edited by James M. Houston. Eastbourne, Sussex, UK: Victor/ Cook Communications, 2005.

Packer, J.I., *Knowing God*. Downers Grove, IL: InterVarsity Press, 1973.

Pascal, Blaise, *Penseés*, translated by A.J. Krailsheimer. London: Penguin, 1966.

———. *Penseés*, in *Devotional Classics: Selected Readings for Individuals and Groups*, edited by Richard J. Foster and James Bryan Smith. San Francisco: HarperSanFrancisco, 2005.

Pink, A.W., *The Doctrine of Sanctification*. Geanies House, Fearn, Ross-shire, Great Britain: Christian Focus, 1998.

Piper, John, *Desiring God: Meditations of a Christian Hedonist*. Sisters, OR: Multnomah, 1986.

———. *Future Grace*. Sisters, OR: Multnoma, 1995.

Plantinga, Cornelius, Jr., *Not the Way It's Supposed to be: A breviary of Sin*. Grand Rapids: Eerdmans, 1995.

Phillips, J.B., *New Testament in Modern English*. New York: Touchstone/Simon & Schuster, 1972.

Reumann, John Henry Paul, *Variety and Unity in New Testament Thought*. Oxford: Oxford University Press, 1991.

Rogers, Timothy, *Trouble of Mind and the Disease of Melancholy: Written for Us of Such As Are or Have Been Exercised by the Same*, edited by Don Kistler. Morgan, PA: Soli Deo Gloria Publications, 2002.

Ruth, Michael, *Shadow Work: A New Guide to Spiritual and Psychological Growth*. Knoxville: Growth Solutions, 1999.

Ryle, John Charles, *Holiness: Its Nature, Hindrances, Difficulties, and Roots*. Darlington, UK: Evangelical Press, 1979.

Sayers, Dorothy L., *Introductory Papers on Dante*, Vol. 1. Eugene, OR: Wipf and Stock, 2006 (reprint of the 1954 London: Methuen edition).

―――. *Further Papers on Dante*, Vol. 2. Eugene, OR: Wipf and Stock, 2006 (reprint of the 1957 London: Methuen edition).

Sayers, Dorothy L., and Barbara Reynolds, *The Poetry of Search and The Poetry of Statement: And Other Posthumous Essays on Literature, Religion and Language by Dorothy L. Sayers*, Vol. 3. Eugene, OR: Wipf & Stock, 2006 (reprint of the 1963 London: Victor Gollancz edition).

Spurgeon, C.H., *Morning and Evening*. Ross-shire, Scotland: Christian Focus Publications, 2004.

Stewart, James S., *A Man in Christ: The Vital Elements of St. Paul's Religion*. London: Hodder & Stoughton, 1947.

Thomas, Derek W.H., Reformed Theological Seminary, MP3 download, "Theological Foundations: Dort, the Puritans and Hyper-Calvinism," itunes.com.

Wells, David F., *God in the Wasteland: The Reality of Truth in a World of Fading Dreams*. Grand Rapids: Eerdmans, 1994.

Westcott, Brooke Foss, *The Epistles of St. John: The Greek Text with Notes*. Grand Rapids: Eerdmans, 1966.

Williams, Charles, *The Figure of Beatrice*. Berkeley: The Apocryphile Press, 2005 (reprint of the 1943 London: Faber and Faber edition).

Zweig, Connie and Jeremiah Abrams, editors, *Meeting the Shadow: The Hidden Power of the Dark Side of Human Nature*. Los Angeles: Jeremy P. Tarcher, 1991.

www.ingramcontent.com/pod-product-compliance
Lightning Source LLC
Chambersburg PA
CBHW062038220426
43662CB00010B/1556